To Elizab
from Bob.

The Akerman Family:
Growing Up With Salt Spring Island

Bob Akerman with Linda Sherwood

Bob Akerman

Bob Akerman

2501 Fulford-Ganges Road

Salt Spring Island, BC V8K 1Z4

ISBN 0-9739826-0-8

Acknowledgements

A person gets to meet a lot of people and hear a lot of stories over a lifetime. And, as those of you who have grown up on an island know, being surrounded on all sides by water encourages us all to get to know each other a little better than we might have done otherwise.

In my ninety-plus years on Salt Spring Island, I have stayed close to my family and I have met more people than I can count. I have enjoyed many friendships with a wide variety of people, experienced numerous adventures and heard about even more.

I like to think that these adventures—my own and those of my fellow islanders—resulted in stories that are worth re-telling for their entertainment value, if for nothing else. But I recognize that ninety years is a long time. Although I have done my best to remember names and facts, I can't claim perfection. If I have mistakenly attributed an experience or mis-spelled the name of a friend or if time has clouded my memory, I apologize sincerely.

I'd like to give special thanks to my daughter, Darlene O'Donnell, for her assistance in putting together this book. She has been a big help searching through boxes of old photos and prompting me to remember stories I haven't thought of in years.

I couldn't begin a story of Salt Spring Island and the Akerman family without offering my thanks and appreciation to the many people—family, friends and fellow islanders—that have made my life so memorable. Without you, my life—and this book—would include far fewer stories and far less entertainment value.

Bob Akerman

Introduction

When Bob first contacted me, his goal was to write down for his children and grandchildren some of the stories he had heard as a child from his ancestors. During the course of our visits, Bob's collection of stories grew beyond those about his Indian ancestors' life on Salt Spring Island, to include some memorable moments in his grandparents' and parents' lives and, eventually, to encompass some highlights of his own well-lived life. In the process of telling these stories, Bob couldn't help remembering some good times and he was always enthusiastic about sharing the laugh.

Bob enjoys a chuckle, often at his own expense, and the stories he shares in this book reflect his unique sense of humour. He has such a knack for setting up a punch line that he often left me wondering if he was telling me the truth, or if he was sneaking in a joke to see if I was listening. He has assured me that the stories in this book are true, but the gleam in his eye suggests that there might be a tall tale thrown in for good measure or, more likely, that he has left some of his best stories untold to protect the guilty.

When we first began this book, I thought fondly of this collection as 'Bob's Story.' Five years later, it has become clear that Bob's stories resonate with all of us.

Bob's incredible memory of the stories he heard from his family while he was growing up gives an excellent glimpse into what life was like for the early residents of Salt Spring Island. His humourous recollections of his own adventures and his relationships with other islanders bring a smile of recognition to those of us who grew up elsewhere, but shared many of the same learning experiences. The stories

Bob tells remind us of the importance of family, community and history: they remind us of our place as individuals and as part of the greater whole.

Words on a page can't capture Bob's larger than life personality, but I hope this small book conveys some of Bob's energy and enthusiasm for life.

Linda Sherwood

Contents

Prologue

Over the years, my family and I have collected a great many stories and souvenirs of Salt Spring Island's history. Recently I built a museum, a stone's throw away from my house on Fulford-Ganges Road, so people can learn about their ancestors, Canada's pioneers and the way things used to be. I enjoy showing my collection of Indian artifacts, photographs and memorabilia to visitors, but I especially like telling the stories that I heard first hand while I was growing up.

By the time they've graduated from high school, every child on the island has probably seen the inside of my log-house museum more than once, but their first visit is one of wonder and excitement. Kindergarten kids look around at the old pictures, the timeworn Indian tools and the hand-crafted sculptures with wide eyes and quiet interest. Many of them have never seen treasures like these before and the museum opens a whole new world for them.

The children know that each of them will have the opportunity to ask me three questions before they leave and, as they explore, I can see them considering which mysteries they most want solved. Gradually, a line-up of curious children forms in front of my comfy old chair. Some of them chatter away and forget their questions, but some kids listen intently as I talk with their classmates, hoping to get as much information out of me as they can.

Usually, they ask about the Indians: how they lived, how they prepared their food for the winter, how they built their houses, and how they used their stone tools. Sometimes they ask about the land and the community. Clearly these kids are trying to piece together how things got to be the way they are today. They put a lot of thought into it and ask good questions.

One time, about twenty kindergarten kids from Fulford Elementary School came for a visit. The smallest of the bunch was the second last in line. He was a thoughtful little fella and he listened to me answer a lot of questions while he waited patiently. When it was his turn, he said matter-of-factly, “Bob, you know everything. You should write a book!”

“Yes, I am going to write a book,” I said with a smile, “when I get old.”

He looked me square in the eye and said, “Well then, you better hurry up!”

When I turned eighty-nine years old, I decided to get my stories down on paper. I have learned many things about life on the island in the early days and I have experienced a lot of interesting things myself. Just as my ancestors did for me, I would like to pass on to you some of these stories about the land and the people and the personalities that make Salt Spring Island such an enjoyable place to call home.

1

Grannie's Memories

GRANNIE'S DAD WAS A HEREDITARY CHIEF OF THE CLEM-CLEMELUTZ CLAN of the Cowichan First Nation that owned the Burgoyne Bay area before White Man came to the island. Grannie was born around 1845 to Chief Tusilum and his wife T̲altunaat; they named her T̲uwahwiye'. She grew up in a culture that was changing quickly, but even in her later years, when she was known as Mary Anne Gyves, my grannie remembered vividly the way things used to be.

Grannie made an impact on me early. One of my first memories of Grannie is of her bouncing me on her knee and singing an Indian song. The words sounded like this:

Unsa lumpa golie
Unsa lumpa golie
Honey sa-unsa
Sweetie sa-unsa
Whee!

Grannie Gyves and me, age two. (circa 1914)

Throughout the first two decades of my life, I often walked across Fulford-Ganges Road to visit Grannie. She lived in a little white wooden house that she built with her husband, Michael Gyves, in the early 1860s.

If I was lucky, someone had brought Grannie a duck from the bay and, while we visited, she prepared my favourite feast, roasted duck with moon bread, the traditional way. Grannie plucked the duck and carefully set the feathers into a wooden box in the corner near the fireplace. After cutting the duck in half, she toasted it on sticks, just above the hot coals. It was like having a barbeque.

She told me stories as she kneaded flour and water into a thick dough. I helped her pat it into fat little rolls that she tucked into the ashes, close to the hot coals in the fireplace. After a while, I could see the grease dripping down from the duck and when Grannie had collected some of the grease drippings in a pan, I knew it was almost time to eat.

Grannie scooped the moon bread out of the fire and brushed off the ashes. The bread didn't rise very much, but it was good eating—especially when we dipped it in the duck grease! We always used our fingers and ate like the Indians, which was a fun change from how things were done at home and at my Grandmother Akerman's house.

While we ate around Grannie's fire, I learned a lot about the old days, nature and life.

It's been a long time since I've eaten warm moon bread with Grannie. And, unfortunately, I don't get to talk around the fireplace with my grandchildren as often as I'd like, but the things I have learned over the years from my ancestors and my friends are worth sharing. I'd like to do that now.

Property Lines

Before White Man took their land, the Indians on Salt Spring Island lived peacefully, for the most part. On the south end of the island, the Cowichan and Saanich people lived in the Burgoyne/Fulford Valley area. What we now call Canyon Creek came down off a big ravine in the mountain and snaked across the valley. Both tribes agreed that it marked the divide between the Cowichan property at Burgoyne Bay and the Saanich land at Fulford Harbour.

Property lines protected the land's resources, which provided food and shelter to the Indians. Perhaps because the resources were so plentiful, there was little need for the

Cowichans and Saanich to trespass on each other's territory. Even so, there were occasional opportunities for misunderstandings.

About the first part of November, the salmon spawners swam into the mouth of Fulford Harbour, but the creek wasn't high enough for them to travel upstream into my ancestors' territory. Until the rains came and the creek rose enough that the fish could swim right up the valley, my ancestors had to get permission from the Saanich to fish in the harbour. Once the salmon swam upstream, however, it was the Saanich Indians' turn to ask permission to cross the property line. Back then, just like now, some people needed more reminding than others.

Some young Saanich fellas were so caught up in their fishing that they forgot to get permission to be in the Cowichan territory. When they got caught trespassing, my great grandfather reminded them that they had to ask for permission before they could fish on Cowichan property. Grannie and her brother and sister walked down to the harbour with their dad that evening when he went to talk with the Saanich chief about the trespassing.

Chief Tusilum met the Saanich chief close to where the Fulford Inn now stands. Not too far away from where they were talking was a pit that flooded when the evening tide came in, making a deep pool of cold water.

During their discussion, the two chiefs got into a little bit of an argument, much to the dismay of a tiny Saanich Indian woman who was nearby. In a brave, if thoughtless, attempt to help her chief, she stole up behind my great grandfather and hit him with a stick! He was such a big man that the woman's smack didn't do more than annoy him, but he took swift action.

Grannie watched with delight as her father turned, picked up the little woman and threw her into the deep pool of cold water! To add insult to injury, that angry little Indian lady found that her cedar bark dress floated on the water and spread around her in a perfect circle. She must have been quite a sight because Grannie still laughed about that when she was about ninety years old.

Despite the occasional discussion over trespassing, the two Indian tribes got along very well. In fact, it was common for Grannie's family to visit the Saanich Indians at Fulford.

Spirit of the Wolves

One summer afternoon when she was very young, Grannie and her brother and sister were walking down the trail to visit the Saanich when their dad said, "I know where there's a wolf den, just up this creek under a big fallen cedar tree. Let's go see if the wolves are at home." The adult wolves must have been out on a hunt, but they had left behind their three little wolf pups. At first sight, Grannie was smitten. She wanted to take the pups to show her friends. The chief didn't want to take the pups, but his children begged until he relented. Each of the three little kids proudly carried a wolf pup down to Fulford to show the Saanich children.

A fire was made on the beach close to where the Fulford Inn is now and everyone enjoyed a friendly visit. The children played with the wolf pups and had lots of fun until, at dusk, they heard wolves coming down the same trail they'd walked only hours before.

Howling all the way, the wolves followed the children's tracks right down onto the beach. Because they could hear their pups whimpering, the wolves slowly circled the gathering. Everyone waited quietly as three large wolves came closer and closer to the fire. Great Grandfather said calmly, "We'll just wait and see what they do." The wolves circled the fire a few more times and then ran up the hill above the head of the bay, behind where the stone church is now. For a little while, all was quiet.

Then, without warning, the wolves started to howl and bark again. All of a sudden, not too far from the fire, the wolves ran a deer right into the water! "They want their pups back," Great Grandfather told the children. "They've run that deer down as a trade-off. Take those pups along the beach, set them down and come back to the fire." So they did.

The wolves waited near the deer in the water, watching. After the kids got back to the fire, each wolf gently grabbed a pup by the back of the neck and away they went back to their den.

The Indians had a special relationship with the wolves and such co-operation was common.

A small pack of wolves used to roam between Mount Maxwell and Mount Bruce. Sometimes, when all was quiet and Grannie could hear them howling up in the hills, she answered them with her own call.

When the tide was out, the wolves often came down from the mountains and crossed in front of Chief Tusilum's village, across the sands of Burgoyne Bay. One time, Grannie was playing on the beach with some other children when the wolves went past.

Grannie walked as close to the wolves as her father would allow and caught the eye of the darkest, biggest wolf in the pack. The leader, who she considered her friend, paused and looked at her for a short time before running along.

She watched him catch up with the other wolves and climb into the mountains on the other side of the bay.

Not long after that, the wolves began howling in the mountains high above the valley. Suddenly, they came crashing through the brush, chasing a deer out into the bay. As quickly as they arrived, the wolves disappeared again, leaving the deer for the Indians.

In anticipation of such good fortune, each Indian knew his job and, at the sight of the deer, they sprang into action to collect their gift from the wolves. After cleaning and dressing the deer, the Indians took the insides and the bones to a special place where they were offered, in thanks, to the wolves. The wolves waited close by for their share of the feast, while the children back home waited in anticipation for their own celebration.

It may have been at one of the Indians' celebrations when Grannie decided she wanted to become a singer and a dancer. She was quite young when she asked her mother and father for permission. It was not their decision to make, they explained, but they gave her the instructions she needed to follow if she wanted to gain the guidance of the spirit that would teach her to sing and dance.

As instructed, she bathed in Burgoyne Bay and walked up to the caves in Mount Maxwell where she waited. After four days alone in the cave without any food, she became very weak and hungry. That night, she dreamed of her friend the big black wolf. He showed her a song and a dance that she never forgot.

She sang her song and danced at the first potlatch her dad put on that winter. I can remember her singing and dancing for me when I was young. I can still picture her dancing with her feet close together and her hands in front of her, palms facing down. The movements reminded me of a wolf trotting along.

Grannie wanted to teach me her song and dance, but I wasn't interested in learning them. I'm sorry now that I didn't pay more attention when I had the chance because that wolf spirit was powerful and, I found out later, gave her the ability to do things that most people could not do.

Trouble from the North

Not all of the Indian tribes got along as well as the Cowichans and the Saanich. In the early days, the Cowichans had quite a few battles with the North Indians. Most of the tribes between here and Comox were Salish. They were friendly with the Cowichans, but the tribes that Grannie called the North Indians sometimes raided other tribes' camps. The North Indians, who lived beyond Comox and up through the Queen Charlotte Islands, went to Victoria to trade with the white men. When they felt like taking a little something extra back home, they raided the nearby villages on their way. They often stopped at Salt Spring Island.

Grannie told me about a time when the North Indians attacked her family's village some time in the 1800s. Her father, Chief Tusilum, was away in the Fraser River with some of his tribesmen. The chief's father, who had been too old to go with them, stayed home with the children and the other elders. When the old chief heard the North Indians coming, he gathered the babies and the little children and hid with them in the bush. The North Indians hunted them and, upon hearing a little baby crying, found them all. I'm not sure what happened to the old chief, but the North Indians took the Cowichan children back to their village up north. Chief Tusilum returned to discover that most of his people were gone.

The Cowichans wanted their children back and they wanted revenge! A Cowichan chief organized some of the Saanich, the Songhees from Victoria, and several of the smaller bands in the area. They all met at Cowichan Bay at a certain time, which they could tell by where the moon was in the sky, before travelling to the North Indians' camp.

When scouts from the war party spotted North Indian canoes at Maple Bay, they went in for a closer look and watched the North Indians cutting poles to push their canoes up the low Cowichan River. Back at Cowichan Bay, the scouts told Chief Tusilum, who then planned an early morning surprise for the North Indians.

That night the Cowichans and their supporters held ceremonies and received blessings from the Shaman to improve their luck in the upcoming battle.

At daylight they attacked the North Indians. They stole the warriors' canoes and paddled them back to Cowichan Bay where they prepared for their journey to the North Indian village. After quite a few days of travel, they arrived at the North Indian village just before dark.

As it happened, the Cowichan group included some North Indian slaves. They sang the North Indian tribes' victory song while paddling their canoes to shore. So that the villagers would not be alarmed to see men they did not recognize, most of the Cowichan Indians hid in the bottom of the canoe. Their tactic worked because all of the North Indians rushed down to the beach to meet their returning warriors.

To ward off concerns about why the party was so small, Chief Tusilum's interpreters—probably the young slaves—explained that many men were sleeping at the bottom of the canoe because it had been such a long trip. When the canoe got to the beach, the Cowichan men jumped out! With help from the others who paddled in after them, they got back all of the Cowichan children.

While they were there retrieving their own people, the Cowichans took some of the Northern Indian children too. Mrs. John Maxwell, a Native woman, took in one of the Northern girls.

Grannie told me that Governor Douglas made a law, many years later, to ensure that all the people who had been taken slaves in the early days were released back to their tribes. Chief Tusilum released everyone, but some of the people who had been raised here since they were very young didn't want to leave. Mrs. Maxwell's girl had been raised on their farm at Burgoyne Bay and was just like one of the family. She stayed on Salt Spring Island until she died.

Grannie remembered another time that the North Indians attacked Salt Spring Island while my great grandfather and his men were away fishing in the Fraser River. The remaining tribe members had seen strange canoes in Burgoyne Bay and, guessing that the canoes most likely belonged to the North Indians, some of them ran up to the caves under Maxwell Mountain to hide until the threat had passed.

Among those who escaped was an older man who was in poor health. He was alert enough, however, to take my great grandfather's bent cedar box full of valuables and hide it in a cave for safekeeping.

The box probably held treasures and shells, which the West Coast Indians traded like money for other things that the tribe could use. Coast Salish Cowichans often travelled by canoe to the Fraser River where they traded shells, dried clams and things like that with the Interior Salish for hides, especially moose hide, and a type of jade that they used to make tools.

After the raid, the old man came down from the caves with the others, but he forgot to bring the box. He died before he could climb back up the mountain to retrieve the treasures. That bent cedar box is still up there somewhere, buried in the caves under Maxwell Mountain.

White Man's Arrival

Before the first settlers came, the Indians owned the land on Salt Spring Island. They didn't have white posts stuck in the ground here and there all over the place to mark property lines like we do now, but they recognized and respected land boundaries. The same could not be said of the White Man.

In the early 1860s, the Hudson's Bay Company chief factor and Vancouver Island governor, James Douglas, became worried that there were too many Americans in Canada. They had come up from California to pan for gold in the Fraser River, but when they failed to make enough money to get back home, they more or less squatted on land around the Gulf and San Juan Islands. Especially considering the events surrounding the Pig War of 1859, Douglas worried that the Americans might decide to claim Vancouver Island and the surrounding Gulf Islands; he did his best to get British people to settle here. To attract British subjects to the islands, he allowed them to pre-empt the Indians' Salt Spring Island property and sold them the land at a very good price.

My great grandfather didn't want to leave Salt Spring and he decided that he wasn't going to have anything to do with the White Man taking his property. In the end, he had little choice. He could see that he was going to lose his land one way or the other, so when Douglas promised to compensate him for it, the chief agreed. As Douglas had insisted, Chief Tusilum moved with his people from Salt Spring Island to the Cowichan reserve that the government had created at Cowichan Bay on Vancouver Island. From the reserve, Chief Tusilum asked for the promised payment repeatedly, but the government kept putting him off and putting him off. He never got anything for his land.

The history books say that the first white men on Salt Spring Island had trouble with the Indians. Considering how their land was taken from them, it would be understandable that the Indians might want to hurt the White Man. But, if you think about it, the stories about marauding Indians just don't make any sense at all.

There were many more Indians than there were settlers in those days. There were so many Indians around here back then that they could have wiped out all the settlers, including the white people, in no time! And since there wasn't any formal law and order on the island, the settlers didn't have much protection. If there was any trouble with the Indians, the settlers had to ask for help from Victoria. By the time the government sent in a warship, which was all they could do, the trouble might be long over. If the Indians wanted to wipe out the new settlers, they could have done it in a day!

Despite the fact that there was no proof that the Indians ever killed anybody on Salt Spring Island, the government was pretty harsh with the Indians. In all fairness, the government was harsh with everyone in those days—when there was proof. If they had proof that a white man had killed another white man, he'd be taken to Victoria and hanged. Maybe the problem was that they didn't need as much proof to hang an Indian. Under those circumstances, why wouldn't a white man blame his crimes on an Indian? The Indians provided a good way for the white folks to get out of trouble.

In any race there is always somebody who is no good. And that's still true now—every night somebody gets murdered in Vancouver, in Victoria even. You get good and bad in every race. It was the same with the Indians and the settlers.

My second cousin, Ben George, from the Cowichan First Nation, sent me a thought-provoking plaque that claims to remind us of an old Indian philosophy: It says:

When the White Man discovered this country
Indians were running it.
No taxes or debt
Women did all the work.
White Man thought he could improve on a system like that.

2

In Search of a Better Life

ALTHOUGH THEY CAME FROM VERY DIFFERENT BACKGROUNDS and travelled separate paths to arrive on Salt Spring Island, coincidentally, both of my grandfathers, Joseph Akerman and Michael Gyves, left their homelands in 1855 to seek a better life in the New World.

These young men were not alone in their quest. Between 1846 and 1855, more than two million Europeans left home for North America. Their journey across the Atlantic was not for the faint of heart. The packet ships they boarded were often filled beyond capacity by companies intent on making as much profit as possible from their scheduled runs.

Hundreds of passengers, referred to as 'steerage,' had to travel in the dark crowded holds of the ship where they ate, slept and passed the time for up to forty days before reaching their destination. The close quarters of the ship, almost complete lack of airflow and extremely limited facilities increased the passengers' risk of catching contagious diseases, such as cholera and typhus.

Fortunately for my grandfathers, conditions on board these ships in the 1850s had improved from even a decade earlier when 10-25 percent of the travellers died before they reached their destination. Despite the hardships involved with the journey, it was frequently travelled. More than one thousand ships left England for North America in 1853.

The Gyves Brothers

When my grandfather, Michael Gyves, was seventeen, he left Wicklow, Ireland with his brothers John and Jim. Ireland was still suffering from the potato famine, as well as the social and political problems that contributed to it. Potatoes had been the main food source for the Irish when a fungus attacked the crops in the 1840s. Although other food was available, it was priced far too high for most people to afford. Before the potato blight had run its course, as many as two million people died from starvation and disease.

To make matters worse, it was extremely difficult to find work. Whenever the Gyves brothers heard that work was available, they'd arrive at the place only to see a notice in the window advising that "Catholics Need Not Apply." Seeing no future for themselves in Ireland, the brothers left their family and sailed to North America.

When they landed in New York, John found work right away, but my grandfather and Jim kept travelling westward.

Comstock Silver Mines

Jim got a job in the Comstock silver mines in Nevada where he was a hard rock miner for several years. Approximately five thousand men worked around the silver mines at that time and, according to a chap who worked with him in the mines, Jim was one of the strongest ones there.

During the 1800s, it was common for miners to work underground for ten or more hours each day, six days a week. Over the years, many miners developed a breathing disorder called black lung that resulted from a gradual buildup of dust in their lungs.

The dust was too much for Jim and black lung gradually made it harder and harder for him to breathe. When he could no longer work, Jim managed to travel to Salt Spring Island for one last visit with his brother before he returned to Ireland in 1910. Jim died from a disease caused directly by the work he travelled around the world to find.

The Great Frontier

While Jim was still working in the mines, Grandfather Gyves joined the American Army and found himself out on the great frontier. By that time, the Oregon Trail, which was first travelled by explorers and fur traders, had become the only practical way for settlers with wagons carrying their tools, livestock and supplies to cross the mountains into Oregon, California, Utah, Colorado and Montana. Grandfather travelled back and forth along the Trail several times as part of the Army's efforts to support the western expansion of the United States by protecting the settlers.

The 3,200 km (2,000 mile) trail wound through prairies, river valleys, deserts and mountains. With oxen, horses or mules pulling their prairie schooner wagons, most pioneers could travel only about fifteen miles each day. A slow wagon ride would have been a luxury for those who walked the full distance barefoot! Throughout the six-month journey, pioneers faced the threat of disease, starvation, accidents and, occasionally, Indian attacks. Between 1843 and 1869, when the transcontinental railroad was completed, more than half a million people braved the challenge of the Oregon Trail in search of farmland, gold and adventure. One of every ten of those pioneers died before they reached their destination.

The Pig War

By 1859 when the first settlers were arriving on Salt Spring Island, my grandfather was a sergeant in the 9th U.S. Infantry. Captain George E. Pickett called his company to what is now called San Juan Island in response to a problem there.

At the time, no one was quite sure who owned San Juan Island—the Britons or the Americans. This uncertainty came to a head when Lyman Cutlar, an American settler, shot a pig that was rooting in his garden. This pig had belonged to the Hudson's Bay Company. When British authorities threatened to arrest Cutlar for killing the pig, the Americans on the island asked for protection from the U.S. Military.

What started with the shooting of a pig almost built into a war between Britain and the United States. In recognition of the event that caused all the trouble, this time is referred to as the Pig War.

Any battle on the island would have been difficult for the British to contain because they were far outnumbered by the Americans. Likely, military conflict would have also threatened the British settlement on Vancouver Island where many American gold miners had taken up residence.

No one had started fighting when Grandfather Gyves got to San Juan Island, but the farmers were upset. The situation got worse while Grandfather was helping to build the American camp in the south end.

Governor Douglas had ordered three British warships over to the north end of the island. The Americans on San Juan Island found out about this before the ships arrived. To officially claim the land, Grandfather and two of his men walked all night until they reached the north end of the island at daylight and raised the American flag.

The British, who had reached the island during the night, awoke to see the American flag on the beach. When they sent a delegation from the boat to talk to him, my grandfather told them, “This is American territory,” and gestured towards the flag. Because they couldn’t do anything about it, the British sailed back to Victoria to get further orders from Douglas.

Grandfather Gyves went back to work preparing the American camp and trusted the higher officials to sort out the details.

Eventually General Winfield Scott, the commanding general of the US Army, got involved. In cooperation with Governor Douglas, it was agreed that token forces from Britain and the United States would occupy San Juan Island until a final settlement could be reached. This wasn’t perfect, but at least it settled things down so there wasn’t any shooting.

Grandfather Gyves was there for another year, during which time the Americans and Britons continued to argue back and forth about the line. Although the history books make it sound like an explosive affair, Grandfather said that the closest the two sides ever got to fighting was during the soccer games they played against each other.

In 1871, when Great Britain and the United States signed the Treaty of Washington, the decision about San Juan Island was referred to Germany’s Kaiser Wilhem I. In 1872 he ruled in favour of the United States and San Juan Island became American territory. By this time, Grandfather Gyves was already happily settled on Salt Spring Island.

Prospecting

Grandfather left the army in the early 1860s, lured by the prospect of gold in the Cariboo. Having had no success finding his fortune, he used his carpentry skills to build houses in Barkerville for those who had had more luck than he did. He must have done all right as a carpenter because he managed to leave Barkerville regularly to do some travelling.

On one of his trips to Victoria, Grandfather Gyves met a fellow Irishman, Mr. John Maxwell, who told him about the good land on Salt Spring Island. "It's a reasonable price, too, so you should come up and look at it," Mr. Maxwell advised.

Chief Tusilum's Land

In 1863 Grandfather Gyves pre-empted some of Chief Tusilum's land, as had my Granddad Joseph Akerman and Mr. John Maxwell. Among them, they had several hundred acres of land that had once belonged to the Cowichans. All three men let the Indians carry on hunting and fishing on their property and got along very well with them.

In fact Grannie and her family walked through the Gyves place often. Grandfather Gyves often invited them into his log cabin for lunch. Around that time it must have occurred to him that he needed some help. When Grannie was about seventeen years old, Grandfather asked Chief Tusilum for permission to marry his daughter.

Michael and T̲uwahwiye' Gyves

In those days, courtship and marriage were quite different from what they are now. I'm not sure what sort of ceremony they had, if any, but Grandfather and Grannie considered themselves to be man and wife.

At that time, Grannie was known as T̲uwahwiye' and had to take an English name before she could be baptized and married. She was called Mary Anne. Most likely,

Grandfather Gyves picked that name in honour of his mother, Mary Ellen, who was still in Ireland.

Together, Grandfather and Grannie raised three children:

- my mother, Ellen,
- Michael, and
- Mary Katherine.

Victoria experienced a big building boom throughout the early 1860s. Grandfather Gyves took advantage of the cedar trees on his property. He cut them down into shake bolts from which he made roofing shakes. He piled the roofing shakes into a big canoe and paddled down to Cadboro Bay. From there, the shakes were taken to Victoria by oxen and sleigh, an arrangement they called a 'stone boat.' He sold the shakes faster than he could make them.

Between the need for cedar and farmland, my grandparents cleared a lot of property. In those days they used oxen to clear trees, move rocks and plow fields. This was all new to Grannie. She remembered well the first time that her new husband asked her to help steer the oxen. You should always plow a straight line, but at that time, Grannie was unsure about what to do and asked, "Well, where do I steer?"

Grandfather Gyves was very encouraging: "Oh, steer it any place," he said. "It's all got to be plowed!"

Mary Ann Gyves (circa 1864)

Michael Gyves Sr. (circa 1864)

Delivering Babies

Grannie's inexperience with plowing certainly didn't reflect on her knowledge of other aspects of life on the island. She was well liked and well respected for her knowledge of many things.

In the early days when they didn't have any doctors or nurses on the island, Grannie was the midwife in the Fulford area. There was no hospital, so she travelled to the homes of the women who were about to give birth. She brought me and most of our family into the world. In fact, she helped bring in most of the children in this area. She was proud that she never lost a single baby.

One day Grannie was hurrying down the road carrying a large paper bag that most likely contained clean towels. She passed a local lady with her five year old daughter. When she didn't stop to chat like she usually did, the young girl noticed and asked her mother why Grannie was in such a hurry. Her mother answered that she was probably going to deliver a baby. The little girl looked puzzled. After thinking for a while, she asked, "Why has Grannie got the baby in a paper sack?"

☙ Jim Akerman, Michael Gyves Sr., Michael Gyves Jr., Tom Jackson and George Edward (Ted) Akerman bringing in the hay at the Gyves Farm, which was where the Fulford Fire Hall now stands. The Akerman family home, where my brother and sisters and I were born, is in the background. The house is now known as the White House. (circa 1910)

☙ Michael Gyves Sr. with my sister, Molly, and Jim Gyves Sr. (circa 1920)

Joseph Akerman

My granddad, Joseph Akerman, came from a working-class family in Chirton, Wiltshire, England. His father, Johnathon, had a gristmill that had been run by the family for generations, but Joseph dreamed of owning land. A farm in England was out of reach for this seventeen year old. However, he had heard that land was available pretty cheap in Canada. On November 9th, 1855 he set off on the *Tynemouth*, bound for Canada.

The Akerman family home in Chirton, Wiltshire, England. (circa 1960)

Gardening in Victoria

When the *Tynemouth* docked in San Francisco, Granddad Akerman wanted to stay, but could not afford the expensive land prices. He got back on board and sailed to Victoria. Eventually Granddad settled on a patch of rented land where the Parliament Buildings now stand. He had done a lot of gardening for his father in England, so he knew what he was doing when he planted a garden and sold his vegetables to the locals. While the garden was growing, he worked at the docks in Victoria and New Westminster as a longshoreman, loading timbers on the sailing ships.

More of Chief Tusilum's Land

In 1862 Granddad Akerman pre-empted some good land part-way up the Fulford Valley on either side of the creek. He must have started building his first log cabin in the summer: before the year was out he learned that the location he had picked, in the shadows of Mount Bruce, was not suitable in the rainy season. Nonetheless, he had already begun planting in anticipation of future harvests. You can still pick fruit from the apple and pear trees growing near the site of his first house.

The Clay Sisters

While Granddad was building his log cabin, a wealthy philanthropist in England was hearing news about the pioneers in Canada and how many single men were in search of wives. Angela Burdett Coutts donated money to the Church of England to help women from England find husbands in the New World. The first group of ladies travelled on board the *Tynemouth* in 1862. My grandmother, Martha, and her sisters Fanny and Emma Clay from Hinckley, Leicestershire were some of the thirty-six hopeful and adventuresome ladies on board the next bride ship, the *Robert Lowe.*

The Clay sisters' home in Hinckley, Leicestershire was nothing like the west coast of our province in 1862. Hinckley was a well-established town whose economy relied on the manufacture of hosiery. In the early 1800s, hosiery was the town's main source of employment, but working conditions were very poor. The situation went from bad to worse in the early 1830s after the Napoleonic Wars, when orders for knitwear and hose dropped drastically. By the time Martha was born in 1839, Hinckley was in a bad state and very few people had work. Poverty was widespread. It must have been extremely difficult for the Clay family to manage through these times with at least three young children.

The industrial revolution brought new hope and by 1855 Hinckley had over forty knitting machines in operation. New production methods did little to improve the working conditions, however, and the quality of life for the average family remained very poor. The difficult times in Hinckley may have caused hardships for the Clay family and influenced the sisters' decision to board the *Robert Lowe* in hope for a better future.

Martha, Fanny and Emma Clay

Brig "Tynemouth Castle"
280 tons
Built 1841 Sunderlan
lost of Seraglio Point 11 XI 1852
Master Matthew Rose 1850-2
John Goudy had served as Mate in 1848
T.C
Was no longer afloat in 1862 ∴ not the same ship!

Joseph and Martha Akerman

When Granddad Akerman heard that the bride ship *Robert Lowe* was coming from England with a load of young ladies, he dressed in his best clothes and travelled to Victoria to see if he could find a wife. Granddad was looking for a husky girl and he found one in Martha Clay. Grandmother Akerman was very strong—and strong-minded too! This was good because, as only the second white woman living on Salt Spring and with a lot of hard work ahead of her, twenty-four year old Martha Akerman's life was about to get even more exciting!

Martha Akerman (circa 1863)

Regardless of which direction luck pushed them, the ladies of the *Robert Lowe* had to accept the unexpected. They seem to have made the best of it. Some found jobs as domestic help in the mansions of wealthy families; others found husbands that treated them well.

Grandmother Akerman's best friend married a store owner from Victoria, David Spencer: together they raised a family of thirteen children. Mr. Spencer went on to become a millionaire. Both of Grandmother's sisters married. Fanny married a Mr. Stevenson and moved to Kent, Washington. Emma married a Mr. Rourke and stayed in Victoria.

After meeting Martha, Granddad Akerman made arrangements to be married as soon as possible. A preacher married them in Victoria on May 14, 1863. Granddad brought his new bride to the log cabin he had built in the shadow of Mount Bruce. However, Grandmother must have convinced him that it was time to move because they built a split log cabin across the valley—in the sun—the same year she arrived.

As was probably common among her fellow travellers, Grandmother had packed her big wooden steamer trunk in hope of a certain lifestyle. She may have been disappointed to learn that the fine clothing she brought was entirely inappropriate for the hard work that waited on Salt Spring Island. She saved her black bonnet and frilly dress for church.

Traveller's Rest

A couple of years after Grandmother arrived, my grandparents began building Traveller's Rest, the island's first bed and breakfast. It opened for business in the late 1860s.

People who travelled to Salt Spring and couldn't get back home the same day paid $1 to stay the night and eat breakfast at Traveller's Rest. Most often, the guests had come to Salt Spring Island to consider buying land—there wasn't much of a tourist trade in those days.

☙ Traveller's Rest, long after it opened for business. (circa 1960)

Like any good hotel, Traveller's Rest had a saloon where weary travellers could relax with a drink. They also had a general store where they could stock up on other necessities.

The General Store was the first store to open in the south end of the island. Although we can travel from one end of Salt Spring to the other and back again in about two hours, it took the people who lived in the south end in the 1860s about a day to travel by horse and carriage to the north end of the island and back. While my grandparents' general store was a convenience for travellers, the local settlers and Indians were glad to have it too.

The Indians often traded fish and venison for staples like flour and sugar. This suited Granddad just fine. He smoked the fish and meat and sent it to Victoria along with the vegetables he grew on his farm. His products fetched higher prices in Victoria than they did on Salt Spring.

My grandparents, Joseph and Martha Akerman, raised eight children:

- Fanny (born November 22, 1865),
- Joseph Johnathon (Joe) (born April 2, 1868),
- Mathilda (Tilly) (born February 23, 1870),
- Martha Ann (born December 15, 1871),
- my father, George Edward (Ted) (born November 28, 1873),
- James (Jim) (born September 1, 1875),
- Thomas (Tom) (born July 16, 1877) and
- William Francis (Bill) (born June 21, 1879).

It couldn't have been an easy time to raise children and they experienced many hardships that we could hardly imagine.

ଓ The Akerman family. Back: Mr. Cook (a family friend), Joseph Akerman and Mike Gyves. Front: Martha Akerman, Joe Akerman and Fanny and Joe Nightingale. Their daughter Isabel (Belle) is on Martha's lap. (circa 1880s)

☙ The following letter was one of many written to my granddad, Joseph Akerman, by his father, Johnathon who lived in Chirton, England:

Chirton Dec 11th, 1869

Dear Joseph:

I received the newspapers December 5th for which I am much obliged to you. They was not long a coming but those you said you sent last May when you wrote I did not get them. I hope you have received all your mother and sisters have sent you. I have sent you some grape seeds which you can plant as soon as you get them. I sent some wheat in a small bag some time since I hope it went safe it is two sorts one is the rough chaff and the other is some that grew on our own land, but good sorts. I also sent a newspaper with Rebecca's wedding in it. She was married the 14th October to a young Farmer of Grafton near Westbury. He is very well off and she seems very comfortable. Henry Far as you used to know at Nurstead was killed a short time since by a fall from his trap at Worton. He was rather tipsey and driving stood up, and let go the reins and fell out on his head behind the trap. He was taken home insensible, but his mother only thought he was drunk and did not send for the doctor until it was too late. McRobbins of Honeystreet died last week 83 years of age – we had a dry hot summer but the wheat was not a good yield from 4 to 7 sacks per acre wheat is selling 20 to 24 cents per sack. Let me know when you write what you can get per bushel the same measures as ours and also if you have heard from or written to J. Clift and how many nites you are apart. Let me know how many miles you are from the last station of the Pacific Railroad and if it is yet completed. How do your fruit trees flourish how much land have you got under cultivation and how do (you) get on with your farming business have you had any panthers near you since you wrote last. Do you send your newspapers and letters with the rail road to America now. Do you get more land brought into cultivation for growing wheat in the country where you live. Likewise on your island, the potato crop is bad this year there is so many of the diseased ones or dry rot, they are now selling from 8 to 12 per sack do you grow many potatoes do you get any bad potatoes in your country. Fanny and Edward Wells are still living at Potterns and gets on very well with the Public House they have got only one in family a boy. Two years old. Annie is still living in London and has two in family. Must now conclude hoping that you and your family are well as I am Happy to say we all are at present we all unite in kind love to you and all your family.

Believe me to remain Dear Joseph your affectionate father,

J Akerman.

Man Against Mother Nature

Shortly after she gave birth to her first child, Grandmother Akerman had her first encounter with a cougar. Needing to get some gardening work done, she bundled her sleeping baby and set her in an apple box. Grandmother set the box down on the ground nearby where she could keep an eye on the baby while she worked.

After gardening for some time, she noticed some movement in the garden. Shocked to see a cougar prowling towards baby Fanny, Grandmother jumped up with a scream of fright. Waving her hoe frantically, she ran towards the cougar, which by then was staring into the apple box. The cougar stayed glued to its spot until Grandmother was close enough to have kicked it away.

Nature proved to be a challenge for the settlers on Salt Spring. If it wasn't the immediate threat of wild animals, it was the lingering knowledge that the land had to be tamed before its benefits could be enjoyed.

In those days people could not rely on welfare or government support to get them through tough times. Like everyone else on the island, my grandparents had to make the best use possible of the land they had available. That meant clearing the land of trees to make way for farmland.

Clearing the Land

Faced with 335-acres of old growth cedar and fir, my grandparents hired some people to help clear, fence and maintain the property.

When they began clearing the land, there were so many trees that one could be felled along the property line, split into rails and built into a fence without having to be moved very far.

Because there were so many trees available at that time, they had almost no value. The settlers used the easiest and fastest way they could to get rid of the trees—they burned them. Granddad Akerman used an auger to bore two holes into the base of the tree. The first one was bored into the centre of the trunk, parallel to the ground. The second hole was started about twelve to sixteen inches above the first one, but it was bored at an angle so that the two holes joined near the centre of the tree. Most of these first growth trees were about six feet in diametre, so it was no easy task to bore holes into the centre of these trees with a hand auger! Once the two holes had been prepared, Granddad put red hot coals into the bottom hole until the tree caught on fire. The smoke drafted out the top hole and the fire gathered strength until the trunk became so weak that the tree fell down. The length of the fallen tree was then broken using the same method. This very painstaking and dangerous method of tree removal was generally undertaken in the wet winter months to minimize the risk of fire.

Of course, the roots of the fallen trees remained in the ground and had to be removed before the land could be farmed. My grandparents and their helpers burned the roots as much as they could and then dug them out with shovels. Sometimes they used oxen to pull as much of the stump as possible out of the ground.

With the help of their children and the help that they hired, my grandparents were raising cattle, sheep and poultry and harvesting fruits and vegetables from their farm by 1895. This achievement was remarkable for the times, but especially considering how thickly forested the land had been when Granddad Akerman bought it in the early 1860s.

All their effort turned the Akerman homestead into a show place that was appreciated by the other islanders. Granddad was quite a gardener and he planted beautiful flower and vegetable gardens. He also had a big orchard with about three hundred fruit trees. People from Ganges drove their horse and buggies all the way to the valley just to admire it. It took the better part of a day to drive a horse and buggy from Ganges to the Fulford Valley and back again, so people often stayed on the property for a picnic.

My grandparents Joseph and Martha Akerman, Thomas Akerman, Jim Akerman, my dad Ted, Joe Akerman, and Joe and Fanny Nightingale with one of their children on the Akerman Farm. (circa 1880)

How Did They Do It?

You may wonder how the pioneers on Salt Spring Island were able to move large objects without the heavy machinery we use today. Early on, they pulled just about anything with a good team of horses. In my time, we could do the same work with a small truck—as long as we knew the old-timers' tricks.

Often, when something very heavy had to be moved, a block and tackle made the job easier. A properly positioned block and tackle, along with a good strong rope, can be used to halve the weight of an object, thereby halving the amount of power required to move it. Multiple block and tackle sets can be used at the same time to further lessen the load and make moving a heavy object less of a struggle. The following diagrams illustrate how to set up one, two and three sets of block and tackle to move increasingly heavy loads.

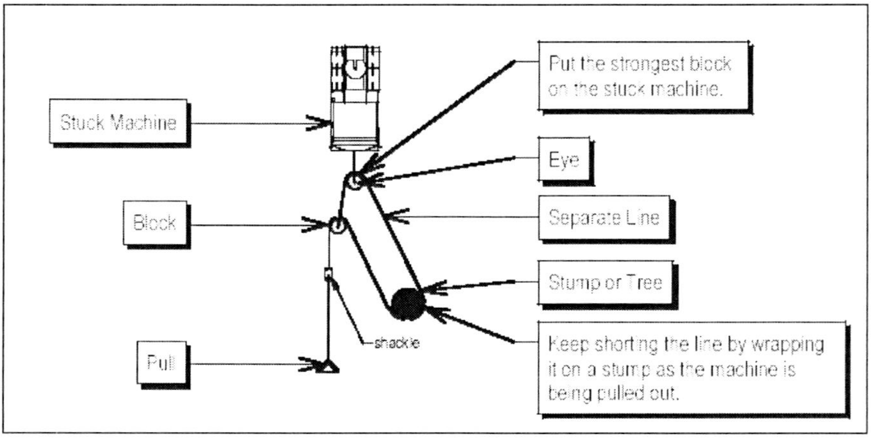

☙ The positioning of one block and tackle to pull a stuck machine out of a ditch.

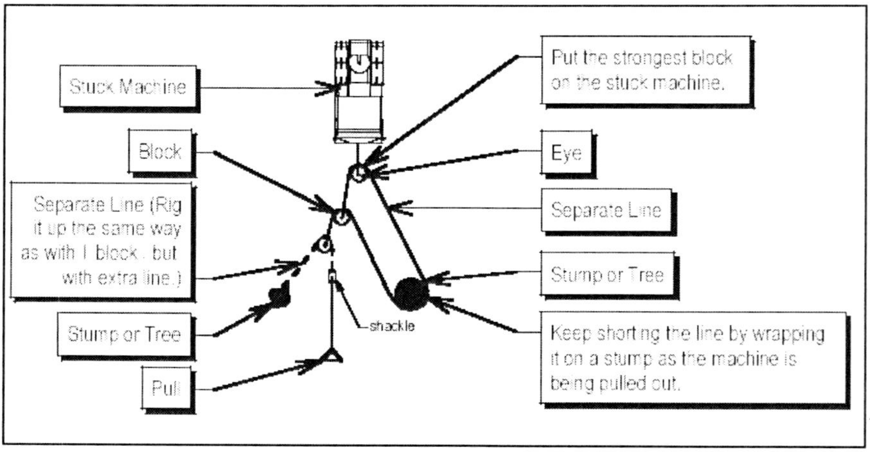

☙ The positioning of two block and tackle sets to pull a stuck machine out of a ditch.

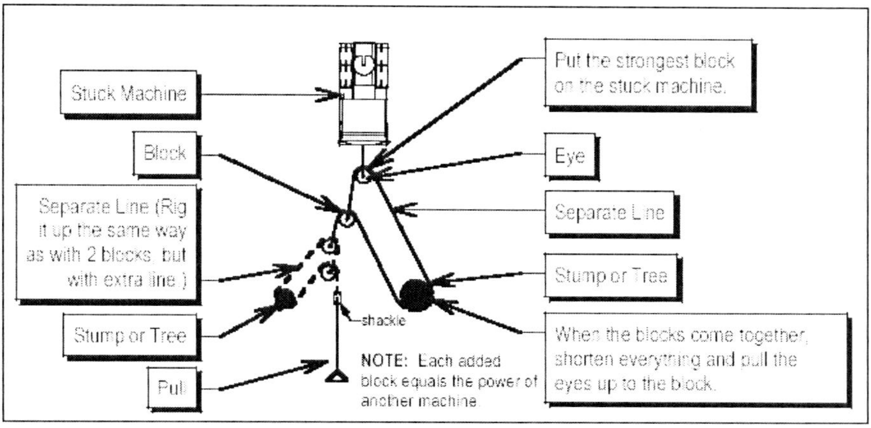

☙ The positioning of three block and tackle sets to pull a stuck machine out of a ditch.

3

Ted and Ellen Akerman

WHEN MY DAD, GEORGE EDWARD (TED) AKERMAN, WAS BORN IN 1873, life on the island was still rough and much effort had to be put into basic survival. Most children began helping out on the family farm or in the family business as soon as they were able to contribute. Very young children got their first taste of farm work by feeding the chickens, gathering kindling and filling up the wood box. As they got older, they also cut the kindling and helped to clear the land.

In addition to his responsibilities on the farm, my dad had some interesting jobs that weren't available to most locals. Perhaps his most influential job was serving drinks to the patrons in the Traveller's Rest saloon. He must have seen some interesting things from behind that bar because the experience put him off alcohol for his whole life. He wouldn't share the details, but he assured me "They all acted crazy!" He didn't want to act crazy too.

While Dad was learning the ropes in the saloon, his neighbour (and my mother), Ellen Gyves, had moved to a convent in Cowichan Bay where she was attending school. Grandfather Gyves wanted her to receive a proper education and, being strongly religious, he felt that this was possible only in a Catholic school.

After graduating at age twelve, Mom returned to Salt Spring Island where, as the eldest in the family, she helped her dad with the farm work. She was quite active clearing the land, tending the animals and gardening.

Not long after Mom finished school, Dad got his first job with Mr. Al Raynes, who owned the only pile driver on Salt Spring Island. Up until about 1898, Dad helped build the first wharves around the Gulf Islands.

While he was building wharves, Dad and Mom developed a friendship, decided that they had a lot in common and eventually fell in love. They got married in 1898.

ঞ My dad, Ted Akerman (seated), taking a break from building a wharf at Vesuvius with Al Raynes (standing, right). (circa 1896)

ଔ My parents, Ted and Ellen Akerman, on their front porch on their wedding day. This house, on Fulford-Ganges Road, is now known as the White House. (circa 1898)

ଔ The White House in 1936, with a new second story.

Working together, Dad and Mom built their house just up Fulford-Ganges Road in front of where the fire hall is now. It was finished in time for them to move right in after their wedding. For many years, that house sheltered them and their five children:

- Melissa Francis (Molly) (born November 5, 1901),
- Dorothy Rita Martha (born November 29, 1903),
- Mary Margaret (Tilly) (born October 31, 1906),
- James Edward (Jim) (born August 20, 1908) , and
- me, Robert Michael (Bob) (born January 7, 1912).

My brother Jim and I are in the back. My sisters Dorothy, Tilly and Molly are in the front. (circa 1930s)

Creative Healthcare

My dad was a very practical man who used common sense and good ideas to get him through most situations. I saw plenty of that common sense first hand. I also heard some other stories, like this one that happened before I was born, that show how Dad made the best of any situation.

One day, on his way to pick up something from the old steamboat that used to call at the Burgoyne wharf, Dad passed by his friend Mr. Dick Maxwell's house and noticed Mr. Maxwell sitting on the ground holding his head. Dad ran over to see what was wrong. Mr. Maxwell explained that he had hurt himself while building his root cellar. He had placed a rock on the wall. When he reached down to pick up another rock, the one he had just placed fell off the wall and hit him on the head. Dad thought the cut was too deep to heal properly and encouraged Mr. Maxwell to see a doctor and have it stitched.

Mr. Maxwell was a tough man and he refused to go to the doctor for help. "That's fine," Dad said. "But if you won't go to a doctor, then I'll have to stitch it myself."

Dad boiled some water, sterilized a pair of scissors and cut Mr. Maxwell's hair well away from the cut. It was ready for stitching, but because they had nothing proper to stitch with, they had to get inventive. Dad noticed a violin and bow that Mr. Maxwell had hanging on the wall and got a good idea. He took the string from the bow and used it to stitch Mr. Maxwell's wound. Before he went home, Dad cleaned the cut well with rye whiskey—the closest thing they had to disinfectant. The next morning Dad went down to check on Mr. Maxwell and found him back to work in his root cellar.

Building Roads

A few years after my parents were married, Dad began the full time job that he was to keep for the rest of his working life. Dad's friend, Richard McBride, who was the premier of British Columbia at the time, got Dad the job. Through Mr. McBride's years in office, Dad had always taken his friend, whom he called Dickie, to various meetings and events on Salt Spring Island. I guess the Premier appreciated his help; he hired Dad on to the provincial government's Department of Highways as Salt Spring Island's Road Foreman. Over the forty-five years he kept the job, Dad and his crews put in most of the roads around the southern part of the island.

At the time, the government had committed to bring a road to the edge of every landowner's property line. When a newcomer bought land away from the main road, Dad and his crews brought the gravel road to the property line. The homeowner was responsible for building the driveway from the road to his house.

On the big roads, surveyors went in ahead of the road crews to survey the slope of the land and to determine where the road should be put. If the grade was too steep on the shortest route from point A to point B, then the surveyors moved the road line to a place where the grade was more level.

Sometimes the road had to be moved for other reasons. For example, when the surveyors put in the road line between Fulford and Ganges, they forgot to take into account the limited equipment and machinery that were available to the road crews. They had no heavy machinery. Instead, a dozen local men used a team of horses, a plow, a scraper and picks and shovels to clear the land and shape the road.

The original Fulford-Ganges Road line was set to go through a swamp, but when Dad got there with his crew, it was obvious that their equipment wouldn't be enough to fill in the swamp and build a road on top of it. Dad moved the road line to a place that he thought made more sense and he and the crew built it there. The best place he could find for the road was still too low in places, so they had to use fill from Rock Crusher Corner to make a smooth and drivable roadway.

Because Dad was building them, he had a lot of say into where the first roads on the island were built. For that same reason, he also got a lot of suggestions from people who thought they knew more about where the roads should be put than he and the surveyors did. He got criticized sometimes when someone thought there was an easier way into an area than the route taken by the newly built road. When he told me about those comments, he usually chuckled and reminded me that the roads that he put in had never been moved. They must have been in the right place after all, he concluded.

After they were built, the island's roads needed a lot of maintenance. Dad and the crew spent many days each year grating out the bumps and ruts, hauling gravel and spreading it on the roads. Many of those roads were far from home and it took so long to get to the site and back again that Dad and the work crew often camped there during the week. At the time, those men on the road crew must have had some of the most difficult jobs around.

Unlike some supervisors these days, Dad worked just as hard as the other men on his crew did. I asked him about that one day and he told me the simple answer: "If I don't work hard, they don't work hard!"

In 1929 the stock market crashed and the world's economy took a severe downturn. Many Canadian men lost their jobs and, no longer able to support their families, depended on very small government relief payments to survive. This time, known as the Depression, lasted until the beginning of the Second World War in 1939.

Before the Depression Dad earned $3 for eight hours of work on the roads. In 1932, his wages went down to $2/day. He didn't complain though. He was fortunate to have a job that paid anything. As one of the few local opportunities for a paycheque, lots of men depended on a few days of road work each month just to make ends meet. Part of Dad's job was to figure out who needed the money the most and to make sure that they got whatever work was available.

Tending to the Family

Dad's job didn't make Mom's work any easier. With him camping on site through the week, she was responsible for keeping up the farm and the house, while raising five children. In those days it wasn't practical to run down to the grocery store to buy food for the week, so families had to be self-sufficient. Mom spent many hours tending farm animals and milking cows, gardening, harvesting fruits and vegetables, canning produce, baking, cooking, making clothes and cleaning for the family.

We had pigs, chickens, sheep, cattle and horses on the farm for as long as I can remember. The cows may have been the most work for Mom; besides all the duties related to tending them, they created a lot of extra work. After milking the cows, Mom often made butter and cottage cheese for the family. Sometimes she separated the cream and sent it to the creamery in Ganges.

She spent many days out in the garden, picking the fruits and vegetables that she had planted and tended over the spring and summer months. And, because we had no freezers or refrigerators, Mom had to dry or can the food so that it would last throughout the winter. It takes a lot of canned food to feed a family of seven through the winter—never mind the many visitors we had, including the priest, the minister and the men who helped with the chores. Fortunately for all of us, Mom was a good cook. We didn't need any proof, but she was always pleased to win prizes for her canning and baking at the Salt Spring Island Fall Fair.

Mom also put her baking and organizing skills to good use raising money for local projects through the Women's Institute.

In the early days, the telephone company on Salt Spring Island didn't have enough phone lines for each house to have its own private line. Instead, they had party lines that were shared by six or seven different families. Each of the families on the line had a distinctive ring, so that they would know if a call was for them.

To call someone, you'd ring the central telephone exchange at Ganges and tell the operator who you wanted to call. The operator put your call through to the party line that served that person's house. Of course, the phone rang at all of the houses that shared the party line, but it was expected that only the person who recognized the ring as their own would pick up the phone.

For example, our phone number was 13Y. If a telephone call was intended for our house, everyone on our party line heard one long and two short rings. If a telephone call was intended for another family on our party line, everyone on the party line heard that family's ring.

One night my aunt telephoned my mother to plan a tea to raise some money for Fulford Hall. They were discussing who would make the sandwiches, the cookies and so on, when my aunt asked my mom, "I wonder if Kitty would make a cake?"

My mom was startled when Kitty, who shared our party line, jumped into the conversation and announced, "I would love to make a cake for you!"

In the evenings, Mom knitted to keep the family clothed and warm. Again, it wasn't as easy to do then as it is now. She had to shear the sheep and tease the wool to remove the seeds and dirt, and then she carded the wool and spun it by hand before she knit with it. She made beautiful sweaters and scarves. She sold Cowichan sweaters for $10 each. She even knitted me a nice warm sheep wool blanket once.

Keeping the Peace

Mom was the serious one in the family, while Dad told the jokes. Even though she wasn't a kidder, Mom understood us kids pretty well and she looked out for us.

When I was young, it was popular with my brother Jim and his friends to shoot rocks with a sling of David. Jim was really good at it and I wanted to give it a try.

One day we collected rocks and Jim explained which ones would shoot far and which ones wouldn't. He showed me how to place the rock in the pocket, slowly pull back on the sling and—the trickiest part—when to let go. If you let go too late, the rock will shoot out the back of the sling—in the opposite direction from where you had aimed it. I spent the rest of that afternoon shooting rocks. I wasn't very good at aiming, but I could put the rock in there and let it fly! Usually it went the right direction.

Later that day I could see Mom through the kitchen window, working on dinner. She had cleaned a couple of trout that I had caught in the creek that morning. I knew that the potatoes and vegetables were ready in pots on the stove so that the meal would be ready when Dad got home from work. It was a perfect day until my bad aim ruined everything.

I had put a rock in the sling, just like usual, but for some reason, when I let it go, it went the wrong way. I watched in disbelief as it sailed towards the window where Mom was making dinner. Through the window it crashed, sending glass everywhere—including all over the dinner she had prepared. I ran straight into the house, knowing full well that I was in for trouble.

I guess Mom could see how upset I was and she knew it was an accident. She also knew that Dad would be angry when he saw the broken window, so she thought of a way to keep me out of trouble. Dad had built up a collection of red bandannas, which he used while working on the road crew. A pile of them needed to be washed and Mom suggested that if I got to work washing and drying the bandannas, Dad might not be so upset about the window.

I got started right away and when Dad got home he could see the collection of bandannas drying outside on the clothesline. He was pleased to see that chore was done and came in the door with a smile on his face. His good mood didn't last long. I don't think he was any less upset when he saw the broken window, but he did go easier on me than he would have if I hadn't washed the bandannas for him.

Giving Advice

Dad's forty-five years as Road Foreman was quite an accomplishment because, in those days, most of the government appointed posts were changed every four years. When the new government came in, they tended to fire the person that the previous government had hired. That never happened to Dad. It could have had something to do with the fact that he never talked politics.

Dad always advised me to avoid talking about politics too. When I was a young man, I used to like to talk at the pub. "That's fine," Dad assured me, "but never talk politics or religion. Stay away from that and you'll be OK."

He was pretty strict about that advice. He wouldn't even talk politics with his own son! I remember turning twenty-one and getting ready to vote for the first time. When I asked Dad for some advice, he said, "Vote for whoever you think will do a good job. But don't tell me who you're going to vote for!"

Dad had lots of good advice for me and he usually got it across in a way that made me smile. He used to keep a lot of his road building tools out in the garage. One day, while Dad was at work, I let a certain fella into the garage to borrow some tools. When Dad found out, he asked me not to let anybody borrow things from his garage.

"That fella you let in there today," he said quietly, "would steal the harness off a nightmare."

Another time, when I was in my late teens, my dad and I were discussing marriage. "I don't think I'll ever get married, Dad. No girl would ever want me!" I said sadly.

"Bob," he said with a smile, "it doesn't matter how grey a gander is, he will always find a mate."

ᘓ Me and Molly with my parents, Ted and Ellen Akerman. (circa 1938)

Community Involvement

While his road foreman job kept him busy, Dad also had several related 'on call' jobs and he was an active community volunteer. As Fire Ranger, Fence Viewer, Secretary of the School Board, and Justice of the Peace, Dad was well known and respected throughout the island.

He was our community's Fire Ranger; whenever it was needed, he organized his road crew to put out a fire. Each crew member got paid 25 cents an hour.

Fire was a terrible danger on the island. It was necessary to clear logging slashes and brush from the land, but sometimes those fires got out of control and burned through the forest, threatening nearby houses. Putting out fires was quite a job because there were no fire trucks or water supplies like we have today. And, because homesteads were often out in the bush with little cleared land around them, a fire could destroy a house or a barn quickly if it got too close.

To stop a fire from reaching a building, the fire crew cleared a fire line, which was about two or three feet across, as far away from the house as they could get. With any luck, the road crew could use an old logging road. More often, they had to settle on a sheep trail or a deer run.

They used a shovel to clear the leaves and debris from the trail. Once that was established, they lit on fire the area of bush between the fire line and the on-coming forest fire. The fire line served as a break point to prevent the fire from jumping from one side of the line to the other. If the wind and luck were working in everyone's favour, the two fires met in the middle and, because there was nothing else left there to catch fire, the fire burned itself out.

Dad was also the Fence Viewer for the Gulf Islands. He was called to settle disputes over property lines. Sometimes a farmer who wanted a little more land moved his fence posts past his property line. After receiving a complaint, which usually came from a neighbour, Dad examined the property in question. After finding a post that marked a true property boundary, he used it and a compass to determine if the other posts were in the correct spots. Sometimes he had to dig down in the area where he thought the post should be to find the piece of china or glass that the first land surveyor had buried to mark the property lines back in the 1860s. If Dad found that the fence posts had been moved, he put them back in the right place.

Closer to home, Dad volunteered as the Secretary of the Burgoyne Bay School Board. He looked after the paperwork for the schools and helped out during emergencies. When I was a boy, I made a special effort to use his resources to educate myself about the rules and regulations of the school board. Unfortunately, the information I got from his books often created more trouble than it saved!

As the Justice of the Peace for Salt Spring Island, Dad signed the paperwork for people buying property. He was supposed to get paid for this, but he never charged for his work. He didn't think of it as a big job, so he didn't claim his time.

Mother was Catholic and Dad was Anglican; they both agreed on the importance of religion. The travelling ministers that came to Salt Spring in the early days were always welcome to stay at our place for the weekend.

When Father Scheelen travelled here from Duncan to say mass at the Catholic church, he stayed at our place. Dad had a cane that his brother-in-law, who was a shipwright in Vancouver, made for him from a piece of oak off the *HMS Beaver*, an old ship from the early days. Father Scheelen always wanted to borrow that cane for his afternoon walks down to visit his parishioners after church. Still pretty active in his sixties, he didn't need the cane, but he liked to take it with him.

On one of his visits Father Scheelen, who had a reputation for bawling out parishioners who missed church, thought he'd walk over and see John Sparrow, who had missed church that morning. John saw Father Scheelen coming and thought he'd better get in the first word. With a big grin on his face, he said, "Oh hi Father, I haven't seen you in church lately!"

Father Scheelen, knowing John was making a joke, took Dad's cane and, pretending to be angry, smacked John across the seat of his pants. John Sparrow was a big man—too big for the cane anyways—because it snapped in two! I have the cane in the museum and you can see the band of copper that Mr. Sparrow used to fix it.

John Sparrow was an active and well-liked man, but he struggled with a problem that he tried, unsuccessfully, to keep to himself: he didn't know how to read. Dad went to visit him one day and found him on his porch reading the paper. "What's the news Mr. Sparrow?" Dad asked.

"Not much news," he said, "but a big ship capsized in the harbour."

With one look, Dad noticed that the front page of the paper, which John was holding upside down, featured a picture of a boat in the harbour.

Dad was polite and very formal. He always called people by their last name—Mr. Sparrow, Mrs. Lee, Mrs. Shaw. He even called his good friend, Dick Maxwell, Mr. Maxwell. This was normal at the time and the tradition carried on with me—even after it fell out of fashion. I had to be careful because I sometimes used 'mister' when talking with someone who wasn't too much older than myself. Not many young people like to be called 'mister.'

Despite Dad's formality, he was a real joker. For a while, it wasn't unusual for someone to conclude one of Dad's stories with the warning: "Don't believe everything you hear on Salt Spring!"

One time, he was telling Reverend Cecil Abbott and Father Scheelen about how the winters on Salt Spring were a lot easier and less severe than they had been when he was a boy. He explained how he had some trouble one cold morning when he let the chickens out of the coop. An old rooster strutted out, flew up on the fence post, stretched his neck out and started to crow. Unfortunately for the rooster, it was so cold that he froze—right on the crow!

Before he heard this story, Reverend Abbott, who had a strong English accent, often said: "Anything you hear on Salt Spring, you have to halve and divide." After hearing

Dad's story about the rooster, he added: "Furthermore, never believe anything you hear on Salt Spring and only half of what you see!"

In 1949 Dad got hurt badly. He was at work, giving signals to help the driver of a big truck back it in to dump a load of gravel. The truck hit a bank, swung down and pinned Dad against a hydro pole. The weight broke his arm and all of his ribs on one side. The doctors didn't think Dad would make it, but he was a fighter. He recovered enough to go back to work for the Department of Highways as an overseer. Dad lived for quite a few more years, but he was never the same after the accident.

☙ My parents, Ted and Ellen Akerman, on their 50th wedding anniversary. (circa 1948) Photo credit: *Gulf Islands Driftwood*

4

My Early Years

SALT SPRING ISLAND WAS PARADISE FOR US AS YOUNG CHILDREN. My brother and sisters and I had the opportunity to seek out all the adventure we could handle—and more!

Cold

I was only four years old at the time of the big snow of 1916, but it remains in my memory to this day. It was a real adventure for the people of Salt Spring Island. The snow was eight feet deep on top of the mountain and five feet deep around the house. That was really something. Before that, we'd never had five feet on the level here in the Fulford Valley.

Our barn was big—about one hundred and twenty feet long and sixty feet wide—and there was a lot of snow sitting on it. Dad was afraid that if it started to rain, the extra weight might cave in the roof. He and my brother Jim, who was only three years older than me, dug a trench from the house, all the way out to the barn, three hundred feet away. When Mom and I brought them hot tea, they were up on the roof, raking snow onto the ground. I remember walking along the trench in the cold with my mother. It was all so strange. No matter whether I looked side to side or up and down, all I could see was snow.

I thought the snow was pretty exciting, but I found out later that it probably wasn't as thrilling for the rest of the family. We heated our house with several wood heaters and, because the house wasn't insulated, it was hard to keep it warm—even without five feet of snow. Every night we cut the kindling for the next day's fire. We had to put it in the oven overnight so that it would dry out enough to make a fire the next morning. Oh, it was cold in the morning! On some winter days there was ice on the insides of the windows.

And speaking of cold—kids today would be surprised to learn that we had no indoor plumbing in our house. We took our baths in an old wash tub that Mom set in the middle of the kitchen near the wood stove. She warmed the water in a kettle on the stove. We generally didn't think anything of it, but it wasn't much fun to have a bath on those cold winter days.

There was an outhouse in the backyard for the other necessities of life. Again, this will likely cause some raised eyebrows when the younger generation reads this, but the outhouse was normal for us. In fact, when we finally had a bathroom put in the old house, Dad refused to use the new toilet. He didn't think it was very nice to 'do your business' inside the house, so he kept the outhouse in commission longer than some folks would have thought necessary.

Outhouse

That outhouse in the backyard got me into some trouble once. When I was about six, Jim and I were playing around the yard when we saw Reverend Cecil Abbott come out of the house and go around back to the outhouse. Jim got the great idea to throw stones at the outhouse while the reverend was inside.

I had it in my mind that all of my big brother's ideas were great ones, so I followed along with anything he did. We grabbed a whole bunch of stones and piled them within range of the outhouse. We fired stone after stone at that little building. Not long after we started throwing, Jim figured out that the reverend would be coming out of there any second. He ran and ducked behind the woodshed to watch, while I stayed focused on throwing all the stones we had collected.

Reverend Abbott came out, looked for the source of the commotion and marched right over to bawl me out! He was very upset and he yelled at me something fierce.

He still came to visit after that, but the reverend refused to talk to me. Jim had always been his favourite and the situation got even worse for me after the outhouse incident: the reverend wouldn't even acknowledge me, but he always brought a present for Jim!

Off the Bridge

We had some other, more serious, troubles at the farm when I was young.

One time, while Dad was out working on the roads, Uncle Mike Gyves came by the farm to borrow Dad's horses to haul some firewood. Dad had raised these big horses, Nancy and her son Sam, to work on the farm pulling wagons and implements.

My sister Dorothy, my brother Jim and his friend Verner Douglas, and I watched Uncle Mike hitch Nancy and Sam to the wagon. I was only five at the time. I loved watching the horses and looked forward to any chance I had for a ride.

When Uncle Mike was ready to go, we all climbed into the wagon for a ride down the laneway and over the bridge to the main road. There was a gate on the far side of the bridge, which was about twelve feet high and about twelve feet above the creek. While Uncle Mike stopped the horses on the bridge, Jim jumped out of the wagon and opened the gate to let the horses through.

The horses had other ideas. As soon as the gate opened, they decided they'd rather be back at the barn. They started to turn around—wagon and all—on the bridge. Of course, there wasn't enough room and the wagon tipped over the side of the bridge. As soon as it got over the side, its weight started to drag it—and the horses—down towards the creek. In a panic, the horses scrambled to stay on the bridge and everyone jumped out—except Verner and me.

I was left alone soon after when Verner jumped for his life. I could hear the horses' hooves beating and scraping against the wooden boards as they struggled to stay on the bridge. When the wagon lurched downwards, I slid into a corner of the wagon. The wagon was hanging in the air and I clutched at whatever I could find to stay inside.

From my uncomfortable spot, I watched Verner swim as hard as he could down the creek to get away before the wagon fell on him. Being only five, I didn't realize the bad state I was going to be in when the horses fell on top of me, but I knew this wasn't the fun wagon ride I was looking forward to!

Fortunately my sister Dorothy sized the situation up pretty quickly. In an instant, she jumped off the end of the bridge, swam down under the wagon and pulled me out. I can remember seeing those horses scrambling to hang on to the bridge with their front hooves and the look of fright in their eyes. Dorothy was dragging me to shore when the horses lost their struggle. They landed on the wagon with a huge crash that could have been a catastrophe for our family.

As it was, Dorothy was the only one to get hurt. She sprained her ankle jumping off the bridge. Even the horses were all right. Uncle Mike got them out of the creek and back into the barn before Dad got home that night.

24th of May Picnic

Starting some time before the turn of the century, the people of Fulford put on a 24th of May Picnic to celebrate Queen Victoria's birthday. The first one was held at Cusheon Lake, but from then on it was held at the Fulford picnic grounds, close to where the Fulford Ball Fields are now, because there were more people living at this end of the island at the time.

The event gained in popularity and size over the years. Eventually it included a parade that got much of the community involved. Kids spent weeks decorating their bikes and wagons for the event. Crowds gathered and watched the parade march from the head of Fulford Harbour to an area near Fulford Hall, about a quarter mile up the valley, where the events were held.

For years people came from the other Gulf Islands and from as far away as the mainland for the 24th of May Picnic. Most of them stayed for the dance in Fulford Hall, which, I found out when I got older, was always made exciting by a friendly fight or two throughout the night.

When I was young, I looked forward to the 24th of May Picnic all year. When the big day arrived I entered every race and contest that was open to me. These celebrations had ball games and contests like tug-of-war.

Coconut shies was another game of skill that was popular with the kids and adults. Contestants threw balls at a coconut that was balanced on a stake in the ground. A direct hit knocked the coconut, which was also the prize, off its stake. It was a challenge for everyone because the adults had to throw from farther back than the kids did. I don't know how many kids would be pleased to win a coconut nowadays, but we were sure thrilled about it when I was young.

There were races for kids of every age, starting at age two. The races were organized into groups of two and three year-olds, four and five year-olds and so on. I remember this well because I enjoyed the races so much as a kid that I organized them for many years as an adult. When I was young, first prize was 25 cents, second prize was 15 cents and all the other participants got 10 cents each. Every child that went into a race won something. After a whole lot of running, us kids always managed to get enough money to buy ourselves some candy or ice cream!

☙ The 24th of May Picnic. I'm the little blond boy behind Arthur Hepburn, the man in the hat. My sister Tilly is the second girl from the right. (circa 1916)

Years later the community added a new aspect to the celebrations. A May Queen was nominated at each year's picnic. It sounds like a beauty contest, but it was actually a fundraiser for the community. A girl's parents or a local company nominated her for May Queen and then they gathered donations in support of their nominee. The girl whose supporters had raised the most money by the day of the contest was crowned the Queen and the runners-up were named her attendants.

Of course, it became a friendly competition between businesses to see who could raise the most money and have their representative crowned the May Queen. It was a good event for everyone—the girls had fun, the local businesses enjoyed the competition and the community benefited from the money that was raised.

Ted, Roberta, Lyn and Darlene dressed up for the May Day Parade. (circa 1945)

My daughter Darlene was nominated May Queen after her supporters (myself included) raised $1,300 in her name. Considering that a total of $2,300 was raised that year, Darlene certainly deserved the title. Over the years, all of my daughters participated in the celebrations as either May Queens or attendants.

Enjoying Life

When I was young, Salt Spring Islanders went out of their way on special occasions, like the 24th of May Picnic, to enjoy things that weren't part of our everyday lives. Somebody would go to Sidney and bring back some special food: oranges, bananas and ice cream were popular. The steel tub of ice cream was packed in ice and then surrounded by rock salt to keep it cool throughout the trip to Salt Spring.

We never had ice cream at home in those days because we had no way to keep it frozen. Instead of a refrigerator, we kept our food in a safe, which was a screened-in wooden box that we kept in the shade on the back porch. The safe kept the food out of the sun and the flies away from the food—but we found out often enough that the safe couldn't protect the food from everything!

One May, my brother and his friends saw the tub of ice cream in the safe on the porch. Using their hands, they scooped the ice cream out of the tub and crammed handfuls into their mouths. They ate about half the tub before they got caught in the act. They didn't get much blame for their actions because everyone understood the temptation of frozen ice cream. When we got ice cream at home, it usually came in a jar.

Once, my mother's sister, Mary, came home from Victoria with a jam jar full of what looked like milk. Us kids didn't think it looked good, but we all wanted to know what it was. When she said, "I brought you some ice cream," we decided right away that we wanted some. The ice cream had been in the jam jar for pretty near a day, so we had to drink it. Despite its unconventional texture, we were convinced that it tasted delicious!

We had our share of good times and good food, but we also had to put up with some things that have thankfully fallen out of favour. In the old days people thought that castor oil would keep you healthy. Once or twice a year Dad got the castor oil out of the cupboard and made all of us kids take a big dose. It made me gag and I hated it.

Every year, when I saw that Dad was ready to give us the castor oil, I'd protest. "It's good for what ails you!" he'd remind me, time and again.

Once, I had my defense all worked out: "I don't need it! Nothing ails me!"

"Oh that's all right," Dad said. "It's good for that too!"

To disguise the taste, I always held my nose and, as soon as it was in my mouth, Mom would give me a spoonful of jam. It was still awful.

The Burgoyne School

I did not want to go to first primer. At six, I was the baby of the family and I was very accustomed to staying home, enjoying life on the farm. My sister, Dorothy, helped me get ready for the first day of school. She was very encouraging and tried hard to get every little detail right. I don't know if it was to mop up my tears or because she thought it looked smart, but she even tucked a little white handkerchief in my coat pocket.

Once I was properly dressed and fed, she offered to walk the mile or two up the road to the school with me. I was dragging my feet, but as we rounded a bend in the road I could see some of the other children walking ahead. I thought, "OK, if they're going, I guess it won't be all that bad. I'll go too." Soon, I completely forgot that I had not wanted to go and my enjoyment of school lasted with me for the eight years I was there.

These men volunteered to clear land for a playground at the second Burgoyne School. I recognize the following men: Uncle Mike Gyves, Mr. Stafford, Dick Maxwell, Claude Hamilton, ?, Uncle William (Bill) Akerman, Bill Norton, ?, ?, ?, John Sparrow and George Edward (Ted) Akerman. (circa 1886)

The second Burgoyne School. (circa 1886)

The Burgoyne School was built in the valley across from the United Church around 1886 by a group of men who joined together in a building bee. When I attended, the school held classes from first primer to eighth grade—and one teacher taught all twenty-four of us in the same classroom. The teacher's desk was on a platform at the front of the room so she could look down the rows of double desks and keep an eye on us.

A carpenter had made big double desks with bench seats so that two kids could sit side-by-side. Sometimes, an older kid sat beside a younger one and was responsible for taking care of him. Some of the younger kids, however, seemed so grown up that help from an older classmate hardly seemed necessary.

Take Alonzo, better known as Socks, for example. School had just started and the teacher had to count all the new kids and find out how old they were. When it was clear that Socks didn't know how old he was, the teacher asked what she thought would be an easier question—when is your birthday? Socks pressed his eyebrows together and pursed his lips. After some thought, he announced, "I was born when the apples are ripe!"

While they were talking, the teacher noticed a little tag sticking out of Socks' shirt pocket. She was interested to know what a six year old kept in his pocket, so she grabbed it for a better look. It was a little package of Bull Durham tobacco. "What are you doing with this, Alonzo?" she said. "You're not supposed to be smoking!"

Indignantly, he shot back his reply: "A man's got to have a smoke once in a while!"

Strong and Strict

Teachers had to be strong and strict. We had some big country boys and some tough kids from the orphans' home in Victoria who were a little older, a little rougher than the rest of us. The teachers had to keep them in line.

Harry was a big eleven year old boy with a bad attitude. One day, after getting into trouble, he was in the mood for a fight and decided it was time to teach Miss Simister a lesson. No sooner did he rise to get out of his desk than she smacked him right back down again. He was surprised to find out that she was a lot stronger than he thought she was! Harry figured out pretty quickly that it was not in his best interests to fight the teacher.

Another teacher, Miss Dolman, had a way of staring at you when you were naughty. She didn't say much, but by glaring at you from up on her platform, she made you feel real bad.

A kid in my class named Fred was another troublemaker—oh, you never knew what Fred was going to do! I don't remember what Fred had been doing wrong, but Miss Dolman started to stare at him to make him stop—everyone in the room could see it. Fred looked back at her and in an instant something clicked.

He decided that he was going to stare her out. Us kids played this game all the time, but it was unheard of to stare down the teacher! Fred stared and stared at Miss Dolman. He expected her to turn away, but she continued her ceaseless stare, boring into the core of poor Fred. He started getting nervous that he might lose the battle.

Eventually Fred couldn't take it any longer and, desperate for a way out, he did the unthinkable. He winked at her! In an instant, she flew out of her seat and down the aisle, grabbed him by the scruff of the neck and dragged him out to the cloakroom where we could all hear him getting a pretty good going over with her strap.

Mr. Mollet's Flowers

When I was about nine, I usually walked to school with Steven Maxwell and Ray Morris. Just before we got to the school, we passed a schoolmate's granddad's place off Fulford-Ganges Road. Mr. Mollet had some beautiful gardens. In the springtime there were tulips and daffodils growing all along the fence.

One morning, we saw those flowers and thought that, instead of taking our teacher the usual apple, we would please her with a bunch of flowers. We would be in her good books for sure! We raced around Mr. Mollet's yard, grabbing daffodils and tearing out tulips, and took off for school with our big beautiful bouquets.

Miss Dolman admired the flowers and thanked us for being so thoughtful. Feeling very good about ourselves, we returned to our desks and settled into our morning lessons. We hadn't been seated very long when I looked out the window to see the provincial policeman drive down the lane in his model T Ford. He stomped into our classroom, glanced at the huge bouquet on the teacher's desk, and demanded to know who stole Mr. Mollet's flowers. I held my breath.

Steven, Ray and I were sitting close together. Ray, who was a couple years older than us, brought me back to reality when he whispered "Don't you tell them I was there, because if you do, I'm goin' to beat ya!" Steven and I were more scared of Ray than we were of the policeman.

When Steven and I admitted to stealing the flowers, the policeman glared down at us and said sternly, "Come with me." We followed him to the car, sank into the back seat and waited while he slowly drove us to Mr. Mollet's house. We walked that route every day, but the ride in the back of that police car seemed to take forever! When we got there, the policeman opened the car door and told us to go in and apologize to Mr. Mollet for taking his flowers. Just in case we might get some other ideas, the policeman walked right behind us and marched us to the house.

We both told Mr. Mollet that we were sorry for taking his flowers and he forgave us right away. In the next breath, he warned us never to do it again!

We never took any more flowers, but that event with the policeman didn't stop us altogether. On our walk home from school, we always passed an orchard along the side of the road. One day we saw the farmer picking apples from a ladder on the far side of the tree. One of the boys in our group, Ogden Urquhart, was a daredevil. While we stood on the road, snickering, he crept into the orchard and snuck right up the other side of the farmer's ladder. Without the farmer noticing, Ogden filled his pockets with apples, climbed down and gave one to each of us kids. We all had apple trees at home, but it was sure fun watching Ogden sneak into the orchard, right under the farmer's nose, to get us some!

Creating Excitement

They say I was pretty bad when I was young. I got into trouble at school quite a few times, but grade five seems to have been my worst year. I wasn't quite straightened out then. I got straightened out later—first by my teachers, and then by my wife!

One rainy winter day the big cast iron stove in the middle of the classroom was going hard, making the room stifling hot and everyone in it sleepy. My big double desk was so close to the stove that I could see the blazing fire through a chip in the cast iron. I was bored—and that's when the trouble always started.

Country kids always had twenty-two shells and knives and things in their pockets. I was fiddling with the contents of mine and, sure enough, I had a twenty-two shell in there. I thought it over for quite a while and decided, "I'll wake em up!" Slowly, I slid over to the stove. Once I dropped the twenty-two shell through the chip in the stove, I practically flew back to my desk, jumped over to the far end of my seat and crammed my fingers in my ears. I closed my eyes and waited for what would happen next. I didn't have to wait long.

BOOM! The lids of the stove jumped and rattled. Everybody woke up fast! They thought maybe the stove blew up, but they weren't sure! The teacher looked down from her platform, up the rows of desks until her eyes rested on me—scrunched up at the far end of my seat with my fingers in my ears. I was over so far I pretty near fell off onto the floor! Oh, I guess I looked guilty! Miss Dolman calmly pointed at me and then at the dressing room. I slowly rose from my desk and, even though I stared at the floor the whole way, I felt the eyes of every one of my classmates watching me as I walked out of the classroom.

After waiting for what seemed like forever, the dressing room door opened and Miss Dolman came in with the strap in her hand. I knew the routine, so I held out my hand. She hit me seven times and I thought that was it. But then she said, "Hold out the other one!" She must have been really angry with me because she gave me seven more! She raised that strap so high that she was right up in the air on her tiptoes. Oh, she got me hard—all over the palm of my hand!

Miss Inge Dolman, the teacher who straightened me out, and a couple of her friends. Miss Dolman is on the left. (circa 1920s)

Now at that time, Dad was Secretary of the Burgoyne Valley School Board and he got books from the Department of Education. In my efforts to keep informed, I read them all so I knew the rules and regulations for situations just such as this one. According to the chapter on corporal punishment, a teacher was allowed to hit a student only seven times on each hand. Wanting to gain back some control over this situation, I reminded her of the rules: "That's all you can hit me now. The rules say you can hit me only seven times on each hand." I felt smart until I noticed the look in her eyes.

She didn't like me telling her what to do! "Oh yeah? Hold out your hands!" And with that, she gave me seven more straps on each hand! Clearly, I was talking when I should have been listening!

After the strap my fingers swelled up so much they looked like boiled wieners. I thought my parents would sympathize, but Dad's only comment was, "I guess you deserved it!"

I didn't like Miss Dolman much when I was going to school, but, looking back, I can see that she was a really good teacher.

Trouble with Girls

Later that year I got into trouble with some girls in my class. At that time our books were shipped to the school. They were wrapped up in brown paper and heavy cord. My friend Archie Urquhart and I found some of that cord on our walk to school and thought it would be good for something, so we picked it up and put it in our pockets.

On our way back home after school, we saw a couple girls from our grade, Florence Mollet and Evelyn Jackson, walking behind us. Out of nowhere, Archie said, "We ought to tie them up! Let's hog tie them!"

So, without doing much thinking of my own, I thought, "Yeah! That's a good idea. We'll tie 'em up!" The plan was to put their feet together and tie them to a telephone pole on the side of the road.

Archie was a little older and a little stronger than I was. He said, "I'll hog tie Evelyn and you take Florence." She was the same age as me, but she was wiry! Boy, she was strong!

I got into trouble right away. She was just like a steel spring. She got me across the road and we both fell into the ditch. I guess I landed underneath because she started banging me on the head with her leather book bag. I could tell that it had every one of her books in it! Even after Archie had tied Evelyn to the pole by her foot, Florence was still banging me on the head. Archie had to come and pull Florence off me. I got up and took off running. I'd had enough of that!

Hallowe'en Tricks

We used to do a lot of crazy things without thinking them through—especially at Hallowe'en. In grade five we decided that we had to do something to the school to celebrate Hallowe'en. We climbed a tree next to the schoolhouse, got up on the roof and stuck an old piece of burlap down the chimney. The next day, when Miss Dolman lit the fire, smoke just poured into the classroom. Miss Dolman made us all stay in the smoky room for a while, but eventually it got too smoky for her too, so she let everybody out. We never got caught for that one!

The next year my brother Jim, a couple of fellas from Fulford and I tried to play a trick on a local chap. He had a big gate going into his property and we thought it would be fun to take this gate off its hinges. The farmer must have been very close by because, in the middle of our efforts, he came running! When we saw him coming, everyone let go of the gate and it fell down—right on my brother! The rest of us ran away, but it was easy for the farmer to get Jim, seeing as he was trapped under the gate and needed the farmer's help to get out! Jim was pretty leery about Hallowe'en tricks after that one.

Froggie Meets the Teacher

Tricks were popular year-round when I was growing up. Some of the older boys in my class played this one on the teacher. While she was at home for lunch, they found a little frog outside. They brought it in to the classroom and thought it would be fun to hide it under her school bell. They waited to see what the teacher would do when she lifted the bell and the frog jumped out.

Most of the boys stayed quite a ways away from the teacher, but one young fella wasn't so smart. He stood right by her desk, hoping to see up-close what she would do when she picked up that bell. He could barely contain his excitement as it got closer to the start of class.

At one o'clock the teacher lifted the bell and old froggie hopped up in the air. This boy shouted out "Ha! Ha! Ha! Ha!" The teacher acted fast—first she grabbed the frog and then she grabbed the boy's collar. As he strained to get away, she jammed the frog right down his shirt! He was pretty worried about having that frog down his shirt and had a heck of a time squirming and struggling to get it out while the rest of the class laughed at him.

After School Fun and Games

In grade six it was my turn to get into trouble again. Because there was no yard, we played football on the main road. We played soccer out there too. That sounds bad now, but at the time we'd see a car pass only once every week or so. On this particular day we'd had a ball game going outside at lunch and it was tied at two goals a piece when the bell rang for us to go back to class.

We were going to finish the game after school and I really wanted to play, but the teacher, Mr. Alex Smith, made me stay after school. I forget what I did wrong that day, but I was kept in for something I wasn't doing right. It was hard for me to sit still because I could see the game out the window from my desk. My friends were shouting and it seemed like I was missing out on so much fun that I couldn't stand it any longer.

After giving it a great deal of thought, I decided that the only thing stopping me from getting into the game was that window. It was a big double hung window. I had to jump up very high to reach the opening and I knew it was going to be a real long fall on the other side. Oddly, I decided that playing in the game was definitely worth whatever injury might result from my escape. Even more oddly, I never accounted for what my teacher might think about this plan.

I made a couple of jumps before I got high enough to reach the open window. By that time my teacher came flying up the row, I was halfway out with my back half still in the room. He pulled the window down right across my back! Mr. Smith took advantage of the situation and batted me a few times on the seat before he pulled me back in again.

So I didn't get to play. At the time, I was so scared our team was going to lose that I risked jumping out the window. Now I can't even remember who won.

Christmas Concert Clean-Up

Cliff Lee started at the Burgoyne School the same year as I did and we got into a lot of trouble together over the years. Once the teacher picked us to clean Fulford Hall after a Christmas concert. We were supposed to sweep the floor and tidy up the hall, but we had other ideas.

Cliff and I rode our bikes to the hall and had just started to clean up when we realized how much work we had to do. Just the thought of it all made us tired and we decided that we needed a break. A bike ride would make us feel better!

Since it was raining outside, we did the only sensible thing—we carried our bikes up the stairs and into the hall where we rode around and around and around. Of course our tires were wet and we left big muddy tracks behind us everywhere we went, but we were having such a good time that it never occurred to us that we were making the hall dirty!

We knew it was time to go home when some of our classmates came by the hall after school. We were feeling kind of bad that we couldn't stay to clean up, but Socks made us feel worse when he announced that he was going to tell on us. That was the last thing we needed, so we pushed him into a big mud puddle. Socks got real wet! And real angry! He yelled, "You kids are going to be in big trouble now!" and ran home to tell his mother.

His mother must have sent word to the teacher because the next day Miss Simister ordered Cliff and I into the cloakroom. We walked in and closed the door behind us. While we waited, Cliff noticed another door leading straight out of the building and decided that it was his salvation. Without a second thought, he flung the door open and took off running down the road—all the way home!

I knew darn well that I'd be in a bunch of trouble if I went home, so I waited for my seven straps on each hand. I didn't ask for more that time!

Cliff, on the other hand, flat out refused to come back to school. Eventually his mother had to explain to the teacher that Cliff would never go back to school as long as he thought he might get the strap. They made a deal and Cliff escaped punishment from the teacher, but I never let him forget that I took the strap for both of us!

Revenge on the Strap

Through my years in school I came to know our teachers' straps very well. Miss Simister had two. Her first strap was small and seemed to work just fine, but she must have thought it wasn't good enough because one day she came to school with a bigger one. The straps were made of machine belts and, boy, did they ever hurt! Us kids were always looking to do something with those straps!

In those days nobody worried much about locking things up and so the school was always left open. We must have been feeling particularly brave one day because we went in, found the straps and buried them! We thought that was great. Miss Simister noticed they were gone the very next day. "Where are my straps?" she asked. We all kept very quiet and pretended to be as puzzled as she was.

She eventually got new ones, but by that time we were getting ready to leave school anyways, so it didn't matter much to us.

When Dutch Saved My Life

When I was young, I even managed to get myself into trouble when I wasn't in school! Uncle Mike went to Victoria for a couple days and left me in charge of feeding his pigs. One was an old sow with a litter of young ones that were just a few months old.

I brought my little Indian dog, Dutch, along with me for company. A fisherman had found him on a beach near a deserted Indian camp and brought him back for me. Dutch was just a little fella, but he was very fast.

To feed the pigs, I had to reach over the fence and put a bucket full of grain in the trough. Trouble was, I couldn't reach the trough because the pigs had rooted it away from the fence. I knew I would have to climb the fence and roll the trough back to its place before I could put the feed in it. The old sow was under a big pile of straw in the corner with her young ones. Everything was quiet.

I crept over the fence and started to roll the trough. The pig heard me and came out just a flying! She was a terrific big pig—she must have weighed three hundred pounds. Her old yellow teeth were snapping together like steel traps. I sprinted for the fence, but I wouldn't have made it over if it wasn't for my little dog.

Dutch grabbed the pig by the nose and hung on! I scrambled up the fence and turned around to see the dog flying back and forth in the air as the pig shook its head. When Dutch saw that I was safe, he let go of the pig's nose and jumped the fence.

That dog saved my life. I wouldn't have had any chance with that pig. It would have chewed me right up.

The Miracle

About the time that I was finishing school, my sister Dorothy became ill. She had been training at St. Joseph's Hospital in Victoria for about a year when she developed tuberculosis in her hip.

Now, tuberculosis is treated with a series of drugs and/or with surgery, but at the time that Dorothy was diagnosed there was no effective treatment. The doctors could only prescribe complete bedrest. Dorothy had been bedridden in the hospital in Victoria for two years when she started to complain of a sore back as well.

Dr. Moore, who was taking care of her, took an x-ray and found that the tuberculosis had spread to her spine. He admitted that there was nothing he could do to help her and that her only hope was a miracle.

Over the next two years, while the family prayed for her recovery, Dorothy prayed to St. Joseph for a miracle. Besides prayer, her treatment plan was simple: spend as much time as possible outside in the fresh cold air. Dorothy spent hours and hours outside in her bed on the flat roof of the hospital's tuberculosis ward.

While Dorothy was in the hospital, a visitor brought her a little bottle of water from the grotto of St. Bernadette at Lourdes, France. It has been said that the application of Lourdes water and the intercession of St. Bernadette have caused the lame to walk, so Dorothy sprinkled this Lourdes water on her back and invoked the help of St. Joseph.

☙ My sister, Dorothy, making the best of her time outside at Victoria's St. Joseph Hospital. (circa 1936)

Some time after she began applying the Lourdes water, the pain in her hip and spine began to improve. After she had been feeling better for a few weeks, Dr. Moore took another x-ray. This time he found no sign of tuberculosis in Dorothy's hip or spine.

Later, when I asked Dr. Moore to explain how Dorothy had gotten better after all those years, he said "It was a miracle!"

Long after the Lourdes water was gone, and for the rest of her life, Dorothy prayed to St. Joseph and St. Anthony whenever she felt in need of heavenly assistance.

Dorothy left the hospital and came home to stay with Dad and Mom. Soon after that, a newcomer to Salt Spring Island, Bill Harris from Winnipeg, got a job on Hudson Ed Lee's farm, which was just about a mile away. Dorothy and Bill became friends and eventually married on January 13, 1939.

When Dorothy told Dr. Moore that she was pregnant, the doctor was quite concerned. The tuberculosis had left Dorothy with a stiff hip and pelvis that the doctor feared would prevent her from giving birth without great danger to herself and the baby. His concern was so great that he recommended termination of the pregnancy.

My sister, a devout Catholic, refused his advice. She experienced her second miracle when her son David was born on December 22, 1939. Dorothy had three more healthy children: Clare, Pauline and Peter.

5
The Prairies

WHEN I WAS ABOUT FIFTEEN, Dad wanted me to go back to school, but I didn't want to go. I thought it was time to start earning some money. My brother Jim had gone down to the prairies to harvest wheat the year before and came back with lots of stories about his adventures and the paycheques he received.

I decided that I wanted to go to the prairies too. Dad thought I was too young and tried to talk me out of it. He told me, "The grass is always greener on the other side of the fence—even when the ground is plowed!"

The Adventure Begins

Despite Dad's advice, I went back east in 1927 with my friends Steven Maxwell and Fergus Reid. Mother sent us off with a hug and a bundle of food for the trip. Dad tucked $2 in my hand and warned me to save it for an emergency. I appreciated his help, but I didn't expect to need it because I had brought along some cash that I had saved. Besides Steven had a big $40 paycheque from his job here on Salt Spring. Knowing we were headed off to make lots of money on the prairies, I thought we'd be in good shape.

The Harvest Train

There were no ferries working here at that time, so we hired a chap with a boat to take us to the mainland where we caught the harvest train. The fare was cheaper for those who were going to the prairies to help with the harvest. It cost each of us $11 for a three-day train ride from Vancouver to Moose Jaw. I remember boarding the train in Vancouver, down near the water, in the dark of night. The train was full of men looking for work: my friends and I were definitely the youngest ones on board.

We travelled through the Fraser Valley and into the mountains that first night. I was so excited I could barely sleep. When I opened up the bundle of food Mom had packed, looking forward to the roasted chicken that I knew was inside, I was surprised to see that flies had gotten in through the brown paper bag. My chicken dinner was practically moving! I opened the window and threw the whole bundle out of the speeding train into the countryside. My eyes stung when the smoke from the coal engine came in through the window.

The train ride was our first taste of what was to come: we had no good food to eat and no comfortable place to sleep for three long days. We looked forward to each time the train stopped at a station to pick up and drop off passengers. We would tear off the train and buy apples from vendors who were selling from carts at the station and bring these back in to eat on the ride. Because the train didn't have any bunks, we slept sitting up on the hard wooden seats. My neck was really stiff by the time the trip was over.

In Moose Jaw we discovered that the crops were late. Men from all over the country had used their last pennies to get to the prairies: we were all tired, hungry and looking for jobs. Steven, Fergus and I were the youngest ones there, by far.

Fergus found a job pretty quick, but Steven and I weren't so lucky. A fella at the employment office said we'd have a better chance if we went south where the crops were earlier.

Gravelbourg, Saskatchewan

It cost us $3.50 to get to Gravelbourg on the train. On the way we went through lots of little towns, including Mossbank, Mazonodd and Palmer. By the time we got to Gravelbourg, we were pretty broke. We had tried to cash Steven's big cheque, but no one would take it because it wasn't local. They were afraid it wouldn't be any good.

It may have been a good thing for us that we ran out of money so soon. It forced us to start looking for work right away. If we hadn't been in that situation, we may have felt that we could take our time looking for work. We didn't worry about the situation very much, though. Steven and I were confident that everything would work out all right.

In Gravelbourg I divided up the emergency money Dad had given me, but we knew it wouldn't go very far. When we couldn't find work, we stayed overnight in a hotel for $2 and planned to walk to the next town in the morning. We thought we'd try the city of Palmer, which was about seven miles north and, if we couldn't get any work there, we would go out to the farms to ask the farmers if they needed any help.

In the morning we went to a place where the City of Gravelbourg was giving out free coffee and baloney sandwiches to help all the unemployed men in town. The coffee was real weak, like they just kept running water through the grounds, but the sandwiches weren't bad—and the price was right!

We thought we'd see if we could take some sandwiches with us to Palmer. When we were in line, I noticed that the guy behind the counter looked familiar. He was from Duncan! His basketball team had come to Salt Spring to compete against us in the play-offs. When we told him we were walking to the next town, he cut up a whole loaf of bread and made us baloney sandwiches to take on our trip.

As we were about to leave Gravelbourg, I remembered that I had left my winter coat in the hotel room. We walked back to the hotel to get it, but the clerk wouldn't give us the key to our old room. He had already rented it to a couple of men who had been up all night on the train. They had warned him not to wake them.

When the clerk wasn't looking, Steven and I snuck upstairs to the room anyways. I knew better than to knock on the door, but I noticed that the transom window was open—it swung down to let fresh air into the room. I knew my coat was hung on a peg just inside the door.

Because I couldn't reach high enough to get to the transom window, I climbed up on a chair and tried again. I still couldn't reach, so Steven stood on the chair and then I got up on his shoulders. I was up pretty high! I could see those two fellas sound asleep in the bed we just got out of. They sure must have been tired if the sound of our efforts didn't wake them up! I poked my head through the transom and looked around the corner. There was my coat, on the peg where I had left it. I reached in very slowly, so I didn't make any noise, and pulled it up through the transom. I was a little bit afraid that the men might wake up and throw something at me—or shoot me—but they slept through it all.

We didn't have much money, but with my coat in my hand and the baloney sandwiches in our bags, we were ready to begin the long walk to Palmer.

Palmer, Saskatchewan

As we walked across the flat prairies towards Palmer, we could see the elevator in the distance. We thought, "it's not too far," and we kept a'walking, kept a'walking and, Geez! We just couldn't seem to get to that elevator! That flat land plays tricks with your eyes: with no hills or trees to gauge the distance, a long walk looks like a short one. Thankfully, three quarters of the way there, a lady pulled her car over and asked where we were going. When we told her, she said, "Well then get in and I'll drive you there."

The city of Palmer had only one street with a few buildings on it. At the end of the street was a Massey-Harris Equipment Store. It was Sunday, so it was closed, but we looked through the side window and saw a man doing bookkeeping at his desk. We knocked on the window and saw him look up. He gave us a funny look, which I took to mean that he was surprised to see us.

When he came out I asked him if he knew of any work around. "A farmer down the way was in here this morning. He was looking for a couple of men," he said, emphasizing the word 'men.'

I summoned up my fifteen year old courage and said as confidently as I could, "Well, give that farmer a call and tell him there's a couple of men here looking for jobs."

The shop owner's friend came in right away and looked us over doubtfully. He didn't think we could handle the work. After thinking about it for a few minutes, he asked, "Can you two drive horses?"

I'd helped my dad with the horses on our farm, so I said, "That's my trade!"

Steven admitted that he didn't know how to drive horses. "But I can pitch sheaves!" he said with great enthusiasm.

I'm not sure whether he felt sorry for us or was impressed with our ambition, but the farmer gave us a chance. "I can't guarantee you a job," he said, "but you can give it a try." It didn't matter to us either way. We were happy!

The farmer drove us three miles to his farm and, since we got there just after dinnertime, offered us each a plate-full of roast beef and potatoes. Boy, we really ate! We hadn't eaten a really good meal for a week, pretty near. We wouldn't have cared if we never saw another baloney sandwich!

After dinner the farmer showed us around the farm, introduced us to another man he had hired and took us to the empty granary where we would live for the summer. He had made some beds out of loose straw with some old blankets on top. I was soon to learn that the work on the prairies was a lot harder than what we had been used to on Salt Spring.

Working on the Prairies

The next morning the farmer woke us up at six o'clock, just as the sun was rising. We were pleased to see that the cook had made breakfast and, after an excellent meal, we headed out to the field. We stooked grain from seven in the morning until six o'clock at night—for 50 cents an hour.

We got our first break around ten o'clock, when it was just starting to feel hot. We were happy to have the tea and sandwiches they brought us. At noon we went into the house, out of the blazing sun, for dinner and were back in the fields by one o'clock. At four o'clock, when the sun still felt high in the sky, they brought more tea and sandwiches to the field. We brought our horses in at seven o'clock, had dinner and fell into bed.

That was the first of many more identical days. We were dog tired and our hands were a mess, but Steven and I never complained. We thought we were doing well. We were making real money!

Stooking

At first, Steven, another guy and I were stooking. The horses pulled a binder that cut the grain so that it fell onto a table alongside the machine. Then, as the grain stalks went along the table, strings wrapped around the grain and automatically tied it into bundles about ten or twelve inches thick. The bundles dropped down onto the ground in rows. After the wheat was cut and bound, we stacked the bundles together in a shape like a teepee, with the grain sticking up in the air, so it would dry. When we were stooking, we started work at seven and worked for ten hours a day.

I had never thought about getting gloves for all this farm work and my hands got awfully sore. There were big blisters covering each of them. We didn't get down to the store until the following Saturday, so those blisters got pretty bad. After I got a pair of gloves, my hands healed a bit.

We used to go down into town with the farmer on Saturday nights. The store was open quite late so the farmers could buy the week's supplies. The boss always took us straight home as soon as we were done shopping. He never gave us the opportunity to get into trouble in town.

Too Much Fun

We just about got fired one day for having too much fun on the job, though. On the prairies, gophers sat right up on mounds of dirt in the middle of the fields. Steven and I were pretty good ball players and it was fun to throw things at the gophers. There weren't many stones around though, and we had to look very hard before we could find anything to throw. The boss must have watched us searching because that night he took Steven and me aside and warned us, "If you fellas spend any more time throwing rocks at gophers, I'm gonna have to let you go." We didn't throw any more rocks at gophers, I'm tellin' ya that. It scared us.

After we got settled down on the farm, I wrote Mom and Dad one or two letters to let them know where we were working and how things were going. I guess they felt better about me being away after they knew where I was staying.

Thrashing

After we stooked for about ten days, it was time to start thrashing. The farmer wanted to get his grain in before it rained, so thrashing had to happen fast. Wet grain wouldn't go through the separator. Besides, it couldn't be put in the elevator because it would rot and spoil everybody else's grain too. It's a good job that it didn't rain while we were thrashing because rain would have stopped the whole procedure.

We worked twelve-hour days, starting at four in the morning. First, we got our horses ready: we watered them, fed them oat hay, brushed them down and harnessed them so they would be ready to hook up to the wagon. After the horses had eaten, it was our turn. We gulped down our breakfast and got out in the field where we worked until seven at night.

I drove the wagon loaded with sheaves alongside the thrashing machine. Then I used a pitchfork to put the sheaves into the thrasher. They went into the machine and came out through the side pipe as grain. Once in a while Steven came along to help me and when we had caught up on our work, we helped someone else down the row.

Our farm was a half section: each row was about half a mile long. Because I didn't have a watch in those days, I'm not sure how long it took us to thrash a whole row, but it was a long time. Some of the farms out there were entire sections—640 acres—so a lot of farm hands had longer rows to thrash than we did. Even so, it got lonely out there in the field all day.

I liked being close to the highway fence because it gave me a chance to talk with the kids who were walking home from school. I was only fifteen and it was nice to talk to people who were close to my age! They didn't believe a lot of the things I told them, though.

One time I was telling them about my home on the West Coast and I mentioned how we had an apple orchard. They didn't have apples there and they didn't believe that we had apples either. I don't know where they thought apples grew, but they sure didn't believe me when I said they grew in our back yard!

My Turn to Drive

While Steven and I were thrashing, the other fella was hauling the grain in a tank wagon. We filled up the wagon with grain and he took it to the grain elevator in town. This fella must have done that for about a week when the hooves of his horses started to crack. They didn't have shoes and the hard work was too much for them.

The boss told me to get my team of two horses ready and take over the job. After hooking my horses up to an empty tank wagon, I put it under the spout of the thrashing machine. When that tanker was full of grain, I took it out of the way so that I could back the empty one in under the thrashing machine. Then I took the full tanker to the grain elevator in town to unload the grain.

After unhooking the traces of the horses, I used the tilt under the wagon to lift the front up in the air and dumped all the grain out the back, down onto a big conveyor that took it up into the grain elevator. By the time I got back to the farm, the other tanker was full, so I kept going back and forth. I think there were four trips into town each day. It was a pretty slow trip with the horses.

Between those long straight prairie roads and the hot sun, I got real sleepy in the wagon. One day I fell asleep while I was driving! Another team of horses must have come up the road and my horses thought they'd get off to the side of the road. They got too far over and I woke up with a start when the wagon tilted on its two right wheels. The horses came back onto the road again and the wagon straightened out, but some grain had already run down on the side of the road. Out of my seventy bushels of loose grain I lost about ten or fifteen, but it could have been a lot worse! I took what was left to the elevator and nobody ever said anything about it. There was sure a pile of wheat in the ditch though!

Towards the end of the season, we went to the neighbour's place to help him out. When we went in for dinner, I recognized the lady of the house. She was the lady who picked us up on the road from Gravelbourg. She was quite surprised to see us again!

Long Hours Rewarded

The long hours made the work quite hard. As soon as we got the horses in the barn and had our supper, we went right to sleep. Our only free time, which was on Sundays, was spent boxing. I had bought a new set of boxing gloves back on Salt Spring and I took them everywhere. The farmer must have been surprised to see five of us boys boxing every Sunday, especially since he knew how sore and blistered our hands were!

We were fortunate to have gone to the prairies to work when we did. Ours was the last good crop before the drought and the Depression that cost a lot of farmers their land.

Canada was greatly affected when the stock market crashed in 1929. That marked the beginning of the Depression, which raged until World War II broke out in 1939. The weak economy left many businesses bankrupt and many workers lost their jobs.

Farmers were caught in the middle when prices for their produce dropped so low that they could no longer live off their income. Despite the fact that they were still working their land, they couldn't make a living.

One in five Canadians could no longer support their families and became dependent on government relief. Some people—including many of us on Salt Spring—were fortunate to have the opportunity to live off the land, hunting and gathering food to feed their families.

The people of the prairie provinces, however, suffered more than most. In addition to suffering the effects of the Depression, they also faced a horrible drought that began that same year and lasted until 1937. During that time, lack of rain and snow left the land too dry to sustain the farmers' crops. The farming techniques they used to counteract the low moisture left the soil vulnerable to the wind, which blew it into drifts, much like snow or sand. The impact of the wind was so severe that clouds of prairie soil sometimes darkened the sky over Halifax. Wheat would not grow; only thistle plants tolerated the poor conditions.

Many farmers were devastated by the drought that destroyed their crops and the Depression that reduced the prices for what little product they may have been able to produce. During the drought years, almost 14,000 Canadian families were forced to leave their farms.

As it was, Steven and I each made about $140—after taking out our expenses—while life was still good on the prairies. I remember getting paid in $20 bills that were yellow on one side. We'd never seen bills like that before and we thought they looked pretty good!

I got some other, unanticipated benefits from the prairies. I don't know if it was the big meals or the hard work, but I put on five or six pounds that summer. Muscles, I guess. And I saw some sunsets like I had never seen before; the sun came up in the dirt and went down in the dirt.

Even so, I grew to appreciate Salt Spring Island even more. We had it easy on Salt Spring Island compared to the rest of the country. I liked the prairies, but I got awful homesick.

Steven and I went up to Moose Jaw and got a ticket for the train to Vancouver. We didn't spend much time roaming around the city, though. With all our harvest money on us, we didn't want to get robbed! When we got to our hotel, we went straight to bed to prepare for our long trip home. Early the next day we took a boat to Victoria, where we got on board the Flying Line, the bus that ran to Sidney. From Sidney we phoned our friend with the fish boat and asked him for a ride home.

It must have been a long time since I had written my parents last, because they were sure glad to see us. They didn't know where we were or what had happened to us.

It's quite a country. I was often going to go back to the prairies, but I never got there. I'd like to go back to see the old farm where I used to chase gophers!

6

Sports

SPORTS HAVE BEEN AN IMPORTANT PART OF LIFE FOR ME and, I think, for most of the Salt Spring Island community. Sports have given us all a valuable opportunity to enjoy each other's company, stay fit and, of course, pass the time during our long, dreary winters. I became involved with sports when I was young and my love for the game, whether it be boxing, baseball, badminton, basketball, volleyball—or any game, for that matter—has not stopped.

I played competitively and for fun well into my sixties, my wife played competitive softball into her seventies and we both encouraged our family to get involved in sports. Even now, I love watching my grandchildren compete and I enjoy hearing the crowd roar during a close game at the ball diamonds behind our house.

While I could never capture in one book all of the sports I played or all the fun times I had with my team-mates, I'll mention a couple of my favourites, boxing and basketball, and my wife Molly's favourite, softball.

And even though the names on trophies can't tell the entire story behind the games in which they were won, I'd like to give you a short history of the beautiful sports trophies in the museum. They give an idea about the sports we played and the rivalries that we fought. Some great athletes from our community and the surrounding islands competed for these trophies. I'm proud to display them for everyone to admire.

Boxing

Boxing was quite popular here, maybe because it didn't require a lot of equipment. I carried my boxing gloves in my old Model T and if I saw somebody I knew, I stopped the car and asked him if he wanted to box. We fought right there on the side of the road!

I really got into the sport when I started boxing in the old Salt Spring Island Jam Factory at Ganges. A couple of local boys, Red Howard and Ted Borradaile, were both pretty good boxers. They worked on the CPR boats and when they tied up in Seattle, maybe once each week, they competed in some of the cards there. They got about $10 for each fight. Around 1928 they started up a boxing club at the old jam factory in Ganges and a lot of the young fellas worked out with them there.

The Jam Factory

That jam factory had an interesting story. In the 1920s, the farmers on Salt Spring each put in $10 shares and formed a company together. They started a factory on McPhillips Street in Ganges to make jam out of the berries that were so plentiful on the island. The farmers supplied the berries for 10 cents a pound and a couple of men were hired to make the jam. While they sold the jam—loganberry, raspberry and blackberry, mostly—to the stores according to plan, the men who made it had some other ideas of their own.

While they were making the jam, they drained the juice from the berries and made wine out of it! When the farmers found out, they closed the factory. It was a bad deal for the farmers, but it worked out OK for us because we were glad to have a place to box.

Learning the Ropes

I was lucky to learn from some good professional boxers who knew the ropes and took some time to teach me. My sister Molly dated a good boxer whose brother was a light heavyweight champion of the world. His name was Roy Cliff and he taught me to box when he visited Salt Spring. Willard Dicks was another professional boxer who took an interest in me. Willard had fought Max Rosenbloom, a world champion at that time, to a draw at Madison Square Gardens. Every once in a while, when Willard stayed on Salt Spring with a friend of mine, we all went into the yard and boxed for hours.

Willard taught me a lot of things, including how to distract my opponent. "Say, 'Hey, your shoelace is undone!' or 'Oh, your fly's open!' and when he looks down—ya hit him!" he advised me in all seriousness.

Life in the Ring

In my boxing days we didn't fight in many out of town cards because we had such a hard time organizing the travel. Instead, we brought in a lot of boxers from Victoria and Vancouver. Old Fulford Hall was always packed with people for our boxing matches.

When I was seventeen Red and Ted put up a card and a bunch of us young fellas fought on it. My first fight was against a twenty-four year old fella from Ganges. When the bell rang, all six feet of him took after me! I was so scared that I forgot to throw a left first, like I was supposed to. I threw a right instead and I hit him! He went down only three or four seconds after we started.

I thought I killed him. They carried him out of the ring and it was a couple of hours before he came around. All he wanted to say was "What time is it? What time is it?" Even after that I was still scared of boxing in the ring, but I kept with the sport.

Boxing just gets into your blood for some reason. We got hit all the time when we boxed and sparred, but we never felt it. That's amazing because we never had very much protection. We just wore gloves, no headgear. Sometimes a hit in the chin buckled your knees, but it didn't hurt. I was never knocked down once during my whole boxing career. I felt my knees go kind of rubbery, but I was never hit quite hard enough to fall down, I guess.

Red and Ted wanted to bring in some out of town boxers for me to fight, but in the meantime the local boys decided to fight for the welterweight championship of the Gulf Islands. I was put against a chap named Eddie Ryan who had won quite a few fights. We had a real good fight for three rounds. Quite a few times my knees felt like rubber, but I never fell down. I was lucky and got the decision on him.

After that, Red and Ted had me fight Jimmy Whiteside. He used to live in Glasgow, Scotland where he fought at the professional level and was a former champion of the British Navy before he moved to Victoria and then settled on Salt Spring. I knew about Jimmy's professional career because a bartender at the Harbour House had seen him fight professional in Scotland. When we fought, I caught the decision on him.

I must have been getting better, so Red and Ted brought in a middleweight from Vancouver. I was terrified to be fighting someone who was more than ten pounds heavier than I was! In a panic, I started throwing wild punches. One of those punches happened to hit him and I knocked him out!

I won twenty-one of the twenty-three fights of my boxing career. Willard Dicks thought I was good enough to box in California, but I decided not to go. I'm glad I stayed here. I've seen punch drunk boxers and I know that if I had gone to box in California, I'd be in worse shape than I am now!

One chap who beat me was the British Columbia Golden Glove Champion. I think it was in 1934 when I fought him in Victoria for the BC Championship finals and he won the decision on me. That was the end of my career.

I never wanted to go very far with the sport. I only ever boxed for a few pennies, mainly because I liked sparring better than fighting in the ring. A good boxer needs something I didn't have: the killer instinct. I didn't like fighting to hurt anybody or knock anybody out. You've got to be quicker than the other guy, but you also have to want to hit him. If you don't hit him, he'll hit you!

Fun for the Whole Family

I was in the sport for fun—and we had our share of fun in the boxing ring and out of it! When my sons were old enough to box, I encouraged them to get involved. When I was in my forties, I got involved again by coaching the Salt Spring Boxing Club. Coaching was a lot different than boxing, but it brought its own type of fun.

When we fought in matches, someone in our corner acted as a 'second.' The second normally helps the fighter get ready and takes care of anything he might need during the fight. One night I was second for two different guys in a row. When the first fighter was finished and ready to head back to the dressing room, I thought I'd save myself a trip. I asked him to send my next fighter out to the ring.

The fans in the hall were getting excited because the fight was about to start. My fighter came out to the ring in his dressing gown, looking like he was ready to go. I put the stool in the ring for him and was about to reach over the ropes to take off his robe, when I saw that he had forgotten an important piece of equipment. I had to smile before leaning in close so he could hear me over the roar of the crowd and saying: "You can't fight like that! You better go back and get your shorts on!"

My son Danny was at the ring that same night. He was watching the fights with interest because all of his friends were boxing. At only eight years old, he was too young to box, but he desperately wanted to be in the ring too. While I was seconding, Dan kept trying to get my attention by grabbing my shirt. After a few tries, and when I could take my attention away from the ring, I asked him what he wanted.

"Is there anybody that will fight ME?" he asked very seriously.

I had to remind him that he was still too young, but Dan got his chance soon enough. He went on to a successful boxing career. He carried on the Akerman tradition in 1962 by winning the same Silver Gloves Trophy that his brother Morry had won in 1959, as well as the George Hamilton Memorial Trophy for Best All-Round Boxer of the Year. (See Dan with some of his awards on page 221.)

Basketball

Basketball was another popular sport on Salt Spring Island. Our games were very competitive, but unlike boxing, it was something we could play without fear of getting injured. When I was a young man, basketball was one of the few things available for us to do in the wintertime. I practiced down at Fulford Hall nearly every night.

Starting at age fifteen, I played forward for a few different teams over the years. At first I played with my friends—Ray and Fred Morris, and Verner and Wilford Douglas. When they finished with the sport, I moved to a team that was a bit younger than I was. After those guys moved on to other things, I played with a bunch of high school kids—my cousins, mostly. By that time, my teammates were a lot younger than I was. I played with younger people most of my basketball career. It lasted until I was about forty.

Fulford/Ganges Rivalry

In the early days, we made a big fuss over basketball. The Fulford/Ganges rivalry encouraged both teams to play our best. Eventually we invited teams from out of town to increase the challenge. Because our competition had to travel a long way to get here, we made a big deal of it. We held three games in one night and topped it all off with a dance that included music and a late supper.

The opposition brought their girls team and their first and second boys teams. After the girls teams played, the Ganges boys team played the opposition's second team. Then, because we had the better team, our Fulford boys played the opposition's first team.

The Ganges team wasn't so good as ours was and they often needed some help against the out of town teams. They always wanted me to play for them. Generally, I played two games—one right after the other. I didn't take any spares either! Nobody would believe that nowadays, but I did it.

On the Saturday afternoon of our games, the boys and girls teams went to the hall to make sandwiches for the late supper. As the club secretary, I ordered the sandwich fixings. We had twelve loaves of bread, two pounds of butter, four cans of bully beef, and a couple of bottles of tomato ketchup. We ground the bully beef in a meat grinder, added the ketchup and mixed it all together. Then we buttered the bread and spread the meat over it to make sandwiches.

We played our games in the early evening and Fulford Hall was always crowded. About one hundred and fifty people came to watch the games. Admission was 25 cents, but ladies with cakes were allowed into the games for free.

Post-Game Dances

After the game we washed up and got ready for the dance. We had a big round galvanized tub, almost as big as the ones people washed their clothes in, for bathing. It was about three feet in diametre and about a foot deep. We heated the water in the hall's kitchen, packed the hot water into the dressing room and filled the tub. Everybody washed in that. The floors got pretty wet by the time everybody had their bath.

We always had a gallon or two of John Rogers' wine in our dressing room and our team enjoyed some drinks while we were getting ready. Now they just go down to the pub or something before the dance, but back then we got our wine from a bootlegger. We used to get a full imperial gallon of wine for $2. It was good wine with lots of conversation in it!

We danced until just before midnight, when it was time to get ready for the late supper. First, we made a lot of coffee.

We lifted two copper boilers onto the big wood stove and filled them with water. As soon as the water started to boil we poured a pound of coffee into each boiler. While the coffee simmered, we unwrapped the bully beef sandwiches we had prepared earlier that day and laid them out on trays. When the coffee was ready, we dipped big white enamel jugs into the boiler to fill them with coffee.

In the second Fulford Hall, which burned down in the early 1940s, we had long tables just off the hall. We laid the plates and jugs out in the centre of each long table and invited everyone to sit down. More than a hundred people sat down at the long tables and enjoyed the meal. The bully beef sandwiches were good. Everybody ate them, anyways! We all had good appetites, maybe. After supper, the cakes that the ladies brought with them to the games were put out for everyone to enjoy.

Once we were full, the music started again and we danced until two in the morning.

Softball

I was fortunate to marry an active woman whose love for sports carried on throughout her life. Molly played sports when she was young and, after a short break to raise our kids, she was back at it full force.

When she was in her forties, Molly organized a married ladies team. That team kept changing: the other women came and went, but Molly just kept playing. As she got older, the teams she played with got younger and younger. Sometimes she played against people in their thirties and other times she played against teenagers. Molly stuck with softball until she was seventy-three.

Sometimes Molly's teams found that there wasn't enough competition for them on the island. When I was in my fifties, some of the local men put together a team to give the ladies some more practice. We called our team The Grandfathers. I played softball until I was about sixty. I stopped when my feet wouldn't do what they were told anymore. After I stopped, Molly kept on playing for more than a decade longer.

Molly was a pretty good pitcher throughout her career. Some of the batters she pitched against were top notch, but they had a tough time with Molly's unorthodox pitch. It was an underhanded pitch that rose and then dropped fast. Those teams from Victoria would swing away, only to find out that the ball wasn't where they thought it would be. Molly had really fast reflexes too. When someone got hold of a pitch, she'd be ready. Even in her seventies, she could catch line drives to the pitcher's mound. She never got hit with the ball once.

Molly was in her seventies when her team, The Fulford Ladies, played at the BC Recreation League Championship tournament in Duncan. Molly was awarded the Most Sportsmanlike Player and the Best Pitcher trophies in that tournament. She pitched all weekend and her team made it into the finals. On the last day of the tournament she pitched four games. That's quite an achievement for any pitcher, but even more so for someone in her seventies. Molly never complained about being tired or sore from all that exercise, but then, she never was one to complain.

Molly had lots of trophies. She got one Most Sportsman-like Player trophy and several Best Pitcher trophies over her career. That was really something, especially since she was playing against people who were a lot younger than she was. Salt Spring Island's women's softball league named its Most Valuable Player trophy after Molly.

ↄ Molly Akerman was awarded the Most Sportsmanlike Player and Best Pitcher trophies at the 1985 BC Recreation League Championship when she was 71 years old. Her team, The Fulford Ladies, won the championship. (August 1985) Photo credit: *Gulf Islands Driftwood*

In the 1950s, when Molly and I were both playing softball, we thought that we could put the swampy land behind our house to better use. One summer we drained the water out of the area. When the ground dried up a bit in the fall, we brought in a bulldozer to push down a nearby gravel bank. We spread the gravel about three feet thick over the swamp and leveled it. The next season we had one more ball diamond in the community.

Molly and I liked having that ball diamond so much that we decided to build a second field beside the first one. People from this area play a lot of ball over there—pretty much every night of the week in the summertime.

Molly and I kept up those diamonds for about forty years, during which time they were open to the community. When we turned the property over to one of our boys, he made an arrangement with the island's recreation commission so that the community can still use the fields. I'm glad they get so much use and I still enjoy hearing the shouting and cheering that goes on during the games.

It's good to know that Molly and I were able to turn the swampy field where my brother and I hunted pheasants into a place where the entire community can get together and enjoy a game that we loved our entire lives.

Trophies

In the museum we have a collection of some of the sports awards that various Fulford teams won over the early years of sports competition on Salt Spring Island. They are all beautiful trophies and they represent some great accomplishments and some great fun.

The collection of Fulford trophies in the Akerman Family Museum.

Football

Soccer is very popular on Salt Spring Island. Each weekend local teams travel back and forth on the ferries to compete against Vancouver Island and Mainland teams. Many of those young players might be surprised to learn that the sport was introduced to the island before I was born.

Tom Jackson, who moved to the Fulford area from New Zealand at the beginning of the century, brought with him his love for the game he called football. He taught his friends to join him in the game and later coached the sport for a few years.

According to Uncle Mike, who played on that first Fulford team, they practiced almost every day. If there was a full moon to help them see, they'd even play at night!

The encouragement came from every Fulford teams' usual rival: the Ganges team. In this case, the Ganges team had a lot of English fellas who had played football all their lives in England and were quite good at it. Tom Jackson told his team that, if they practiced hard enough, they could beat Ganges.

Starting in 1910, the local football teams began competing for a lovely silver trophy. The McPhillips Cup was donated by Mr. McPhillips, the Member of Parliament for Saanich and the Gulf Islands. The McPhillips Cup started a tradition on the island that the first team to win the trophy three times in a row could keep it.

As you can see by the list of winners below, competition for the McPhillips Cup raged for more than ten years before it was claimed by the Fulford team in 1924. Like all other things at the time, competition for the trophy was put on hold during the First World War, when most of the players were fighting overseas.

Year	**McPhillips Cup Winner**
1910	Ganges
1911	Ganges
1912	Fulford
1913	Fulford
1914	Ganges
First World War	
1922	Fulford
1923	Fulford
1924	Fulford

McPhillips Cup Winners – Football

☙ McPhillips Cup Winners (1910) Front: Claude Hamilton, Bill Hamilton, Jack Lumley, Mike Gyves, Jerry Hamilton, Adolf Trage, Bill Shepherd and Tommy McIntyre. Back: Art Williams, John Sparrow and Leon King.

Once the Fulford team won the McPhillips Cup, a second trophy was donated to the Saanich and Gulf Islands Football League by the Honorable John Hart, the Member of Parliament for Saanich and the Gulf Islands. He later became British Columbia's Minister of Finance. Competition for the Hart Challenge Cup was also stiff, but Fulford won again in the end, and this trophy sits beside the McPhillips Cup in the museum.

The Fulford Team with the Hart Challenge Cup in 1925. Back: Leo Harris, Tom Isherwood and Frank Downey. Middle: Captain Drummond, Bill Hamilton and Fred Morris. Front: Bill Coopsie, Ed Lumley, ? Turner, Gerry Hamilton and my brother Jim Akerman.

I was proud to play on the Fulford team that brought the Hart Challenge Cup to Fulford in 1930. In 1928, I had gone down to the field to watch them play and learned that one of their players couldn't make it to the game. Uncle Mike asked me to fill in for him and I did. I happened to be wearing my barn shoes, which were very slippery, but I played inside-right anyways. I must have been pretty lucky because I scored two goals. We beat Ganges two-one to win the Cup. I stayed with the team and we won again the next two years in a row and brought the trophy home.

I must admit that Ganges won the last trophy—the MacIntosh Cup in 1935. In the finals of that challenge, we played to a draw in Ganges and then played to another draw in Fulford. We travelled to Sidney for the final game. It was also a draw, so we played overtime. Desmond Crofton scored the winning goal.

In 1936 we joined our Fulford and Ganges teams and competed in the Victoria League. Our combined team won the Vancouver Island Championship that year, but things seemed to go down hill after that.

Year	Hart Challenge Cup Winner
1925	Fulford
1926	Fulford
1927	Ganges
1928	Fulford
1929	Fulford
1930	Fulford

Hart Challenge Cup Winners – Football

Baseball

Baseball was a popular sport when I was a young man and when Mr. M.B. Jackson donated the Silver Shield that was competed for within the Saanich and Gulf Islands league, our Fulford team won it the first three years: 1929, 1930 and 1931. The players on our winning team were my brother Jim and myself, Bill Coopsie, Verner Douglas, Tom Isherwood, Fred and Ray Morris, and Angus, Steven and Fred Maxwell.

Fastball

As we got older, our preference turned to fastball and, once again, our Fulford team was strong. The Salt Spring League began competing for the Kingsley Cup in 1935 and by 1937, Fulford had won it three times and got to keep the trophy.

A few years later, after World War II, Mr. J.S. Taylor, our Member of Parliament, presented a challenge trophy to the

Saanich and the Gulf Islands Fastball League and the competition was on again. Fulford won each year between 1948 and 1959, and brought the trophy home.

Our Fulford Fastball Team then won the Fastball Rose Bowl, which was donated by our MLA, Captain M.F. McIntosh, after winning three years in a row.

☙ Me and a couple of my teammates: Fred Morris and my brother Jim Akerman.

Fulford Fastball Team Saanich & Gulf Island Champions. Back: Charlie Brenton, George Hearst, Harry Greenhough, Floyd Kaye, John Graham, Bob Howard and Pat Brenton. Front: Alec McMannus, Elmer Lee, me, Roy Whitehead and our batboy, Brian Brenton (circa 1959)

Badminton

I was a keen badminton player in my time and I enjoyed the sport for many years. I was fortunate to compete against some strong players—in both singles and doubles leagues. In the late 40s and early 50s in particular, we had some great competitions.

Here's how the trophy competitions played out:

Year	B.W.I. McAfee Challenge Cup – Men's Singles
1946	Mac Mouat
1947	Bob Akerman
1948	Floyd Kaye
1949	Bob Akerman
1950	Floyd Kaye
1951	Bob Akerman
1952	Floyd Kaye
1953	Pat Brenton
1954	Brian Brenton

☙ B.W.I. McAfee Challenge Cup – Men's Singles Badminton

Year	Challenge Cup – Men's Doubles
1945	Mac Mouat and George Heinekey
1946	Bob Akerman and Floyd Kaye
1947	Bob Akerman and Floyd Kaye
1948	Bob Akerman and Floyd Kaye
1949	Bob Akerman and Floyd Kaye
1950	Bob Akerman and Floyd Kaye
1951	Bob Akerman and Floyd Kaye
1952	Bob Akerman and Floyd Kaye

☙ Challenge Cup – Men's Doubles Badminton

7

Coming of Age

I WAS THRILLED WHEN I GOT MY FIRST CAR. It was a 1914 model T Ford with a canvas top. It was one of the first things I bought with the money I made harvesting in Saskatchewan. The car had belonged to the mailman at Ganges and I paid him $35 for it. In those days you didn't need to have a license to drive. As long as you could take it on the road, you could drive it.

I had to turn the crank at the front of the car to get it started. Model T owners had to know what they were doing because advancing the spark too much made it kick back hard enough to break an arm!

Sneaking into the Pub

My friends and I had a lot of fun with that old car!

I drove my Ford over to the old Harbour House in Ganges the first time Steven Maxwell and I got into a pub. Only men, twenty-one years and older, were allowed in the pub. Steven and I were just sixteen, so we slipped in and sat in the corner where we thought nobody could see us.

We had a bottle of beer apiece and we were feeling the thrill of being adults when I felt someone looking at me. I turned around and look-it here was this great big policeman. Mr. Tweedhope—all two hundred and fifty pounds and six feet plus of him—was staring at me with a very serious look on his face. My stomach dropped and turned. The policeman stared and stared, but he never said anything. I didn't dare say a word either.

Steven was afraid we were going to get into trouble and I felt pretty nervous myself. I pulled the collar of my old coat up around my face and waited uncomfortably for what would happen next. Mr. Tweedhope kept staring. Steven and I were mighty upset by the time he rose out of his chair, but he slowly turned and walked out without ever saying a word to us.

I guess if we had been making any noise or causing a disturbance we would have got it, but we were too scared to move!

After that, we went to the pub quite a bit. We could go to the pub every Friday night if we wanted to. We never had too much to drink, though. I could always drive my old car back home. I've driven since I was fifteen years old and never had an accident yet.

Making a Grand Entrance

We did some crazy things in that old Ford.

I drove the whole Fulford baseball team to Ganges to play—the whole team! The first summer I had the car, our team won the league championship. Everyone piled on—some of them were standing on the running boards—and we drove down to Fulford to have a beer at the pub.

On the way there I told them, "When I get down there, I'm gonna run it right into the pub!" There were about six steps going up onto the platform leading into the pub, but this particular Ford had very big wheels on it. They were 30 x 3 1/2—a thirty inch wheel by a three and a half inch tire. With the entire team on board, I swung the car around in the parking lot and, with everyone cheering me on, squared up with the staircase and drove the front wheels right up onto the porch!

The owner looked out and here was a car full of young men right up on his top step! After the boys jumped out, I backed off and parked the car. They talked about that for years!

Here I am with my first car: a 1914 Model T Ford. (circa 1928)

Living with the Rain

Everyone liked driving in my car, but some days provided a nicer ride than others. The old canvas top used to leak. There was a crack in the top just over the driver and passenger seats.

One rainy night I picked up a friend to take her to a dance. We got out to the car and the rain was just pouring down. She knew about the leak in the roof and looked a little worried about her fancy dress and hairdo. “No worries!” I said, “I’ve got an umbrella here.” After we got in the car, I put up the umbrella and she held it over our heads for the two mile drive to the dance!

Dancing

We had some great dances here in the early days. Admission was 25 cents, but ladies with cakes were admitted for free. When I was younger they held the dances in the old schoolhouse. They pushed the desks against the wall and everyone danced in the middle of the classroom. By the time I got back from the prairies, the dances were held at the old Fulford Hall. People of all ages got dressed up and came to laugh and dance the night away.

I was about fifteen when I got my first suit to wear to special occasions like the dances. I went to Victoria to buy the pants, coat and tie. I wore the suit home and thought I was really dressed up. I felt pretty good, so I thought they’d all say how good I looked when I walked into the house. Dad took one look at me and said, “You’re all dressed up! You look just like a new manure fork!”

Dances were one of our favourite forms of entertainment and lots of people pitched in and offered whatever they could. Some people organized the food, while others provided the entertainment. We had a very good orchestra: Mrs. Ruckle played the piano, Leon King played the violin, Frank Downey played the drums and Emily Maxwell played the mandolin. They didn't have a singer, but they could play all the old hits of the 1920s. Everyone liked the slow waltzes and foxtrots. I remember dancing to *In the Good Ole Summertime.*

More to Life than Dancing

I really looked forward to those dances. One night, as I was waiting to meet the boys, Dad suggested that I should cut the hay out back of the barn. I couldn't believe his timing—after all, he must have known I was on my way to a dance because I was wearing my suit and had a fresh new haircut! There were about six acres to be cut and I knew that there was no way I could get it done before I was supposed to leave. Dad must have smiled to himself when, looking for a way out, I said quickly, "Oh sure, I'll be up early tomorrow and I'll cut it then. You go to work and don't worry about it."

I was out pretty late at the dance that night, drinking loganberry wine with my friends, and it started to get daylight before I realized that I had better get myself home. Boy, I was tired! I couldn't wait to get to bed. I went to the bathroom, changed and then headed for my room. But then I met Dad in the kitchen.

He used to get up around four or five o'clock in the morning to start work on the roads. "Oh, Bob! I'm glad you're up so early to get that hay cut."

"Yup, that's why I'm up—I thought I'd better get up early to get it cut before it got too hot." So I went back to the bathroom, changed into my overalls, had breakfast and as soon as the dew got off the ground I started to cut hay. It was a tough day, but Dad came home from work that night to find the hay cut. And he probably wasn't surprised to find that I had gone to bed early!

Living with Hangovers

Dad didn't have much patience for my hangovers. One morning I woke up feeling awful. I had stayed at the pub too late the night before and I was paying for it. Dad took one look at me and said, "Well, we've got to go out and haul some wood for the winter time." Hauling wood with the horses and wagon was no easy job.

"Oh Dad, I can't go out today! I've got the flu. I'm sick or something." I knew I had drunk too much beer, but I didn't tell him that and I figured he wouldn't know otherwise. "I can't go out," I insisted. "I think I'm gonna die!"

"Hell Bob, you'll never die," he teased, "You'll dry up and blow away!" And then he made me haul the firewood.

A Drink or Two Too Many

We had quite a provincial policeman here in the early days. Mr. Jim Rogers liked to have a drink. Sometimes, his need for a drink caused as much trouble for my friends and me as it did for him.

At the dances, we generally had a few gallons of wine or cider out under the cedar tree because liquor was not allowed in the hall. Our alcohol came in big five-gallon stone jugs that were very heavy. We tied a long rope to the handle of the jug and threw the rope up and over the bough of the cedar tree. We pulled on the rope, hoisting the jug up in the air so it would be easy to pour, and tied down the other end of the rope so that the jug wouldn't fall. The boys were all sneaking a drink under the tree when Jim Rogers drove by. Maybe the lights from the dance shone out the window, lighting the area a little bit—or maybe he saw the glow of the boys' cigarettes—because he came by to see what we were doing. When he saw that we were drinking, he said quietly, "If you boys don't give me one, I'll pinch you all for drinking in a public place!"

Many years later, Jim and I became friends and he told me about his drinking and how it had caused him a lot of trouble.

Rumrunners

During the 1920s, while there was prohibition in the States, rumrunners supplied the Americans with illegal liquor. In Victoria, they loaded up good-sized boats with alcohol and hid out at some port around the Gulf Islands—because they were handier to the States—until they could cross the strait to Washington in the dark. Someone would be waiting either on-shore or in a boat on the harbour to take the liquor from them.

Mr. Rogers and Mr. Reid Bittancourt, a Customs Officer, were supposed to catch the rumrunners. At Bedwell Harbour on Pender Island, they intercepted quite a large boat that was loaded down with cases of liquor. It tried to get away, but the harbour was quite narrow there, so Mr. Bittancourt took his boat, *Whitamack*, close enough that Mr. Rogers jumped aboard with his six-gun. They towed the boat to Ganges and tied it up at the Customs wharf.

Sometimes rumrunners travelled with other boats for protection. For fear that the boat be high-jacked from the customs wharf, Mr. Rogers was supposed to guard the boat with his old ten-shot 303 army rifle. Mr. Bittancourt went home to his house on the hill above the dock. Around midnight, Mr. Rogers got to thinking. "Boy, there's so much liquor here. I better get some of that!"

By the Light of the Moon

Mr. Rogers lived just down the beach a ways, so he loaded a skiff with cases of liquor and rowed his boatload home. By the light of the moon, he stacked the cases under a big cedar tree on the beach below his house before returning to his patrol of the rumrunner's boat. Once he got back and saw all the cases of liquor that were still left in the hold of the ship, it made sense that he should take some more home. So he rowed another boatload home and stacked it with the other cases under his tree.

When he returned to his post, he worried that the boat looked a little empty. Afraid that the customs officer might notice that so many cases were missing, he needed to think of a plan fast.

Mr. Rogers stood on the deck and fired shots from his gun into the dark sky. In no time, Mr. Bittancourt came running down to the dock to find out what was wrong. "Well," Mr. Rogers said, stumbling for the right words, "A high-jacker came in. I was at my house getting some coffee—and when I got back, they were unloading these cases of whisky. When I saw them, I just started to shoot! They sure did get quite a bit of liquor."

"Well, it's a good job they didn't get it all!" Mr. Bittancourt said with relief.

The next morning, when Mr. Rogers got home from work, he carried the cases of alcohol up from the beach to his garden where he buried them. Nobody ever found him out. He told me that he was digging cases of liquor out of his garden for three years.

Unfortunately for Jim, the temptation was too much for him. He became an alcoholic and lost his job with the police force not too long after he took the rumrunners' liquor.

8

Living Off the Land

WHEN I WAS A YOUNG MAN IN THE HUNGRY THIRTIES, there was very little money here on the island. We had to make do with whatever we could find, but we were far better off than a lot of other Canadians. We hunted for game, grew fruit and vegetables and raised a cow for milk, but that wasn't any different from the way we had always lived—off the land. When we got tired of hunting, we'd get fish, clams and crab. We always used to say, "When the tide's out, the table's set!"

Nobody grumbled about it. That's just the way it was. We had a good living—lots to eat and a dry place to sleep—but no money! We were just living that's all. It was nothing new for me. I was doing it from as far back as I can remember.

Grannie started teaching me how to live off the land when I was quite young. At the time, I just enjoyed spending time with Grannie, but later I realized that she had taught me the survival skills I needed to enjoy the outdoors and use it to my advantage during the tough times. Between Grannie and my parents, I enjoyed a wonderful hands-on education.

Hunting

I had my first hunting trip when I was five years old. I spotted a flock of pigeons in the grain field and told Dad I would like to get some. He got the twelve-gauge Parker from the gun rack and said "Let's go!" We crawled along the fence line to get in range of the pigeons. Dad showed me how to hold the butt of the gun real close to my shoulder and shoot. I was real proud to get two birds on my very first trip.

Not too long after that, Dad bought me a twenty-two calibre gun that I used to shoot birds out of the cherry trees. It was also my job to shoot any rats that came around the pigpens looking for grain.

ઊ Me and my dog Paddy, getting ready for a hunting trip. (circa 1920)

Granddad Akerman's Orchard

When I was as young as eight, Dad let me go half a mile up the mountain to my granddad Akerman's orchard, where I hunted blue grouse and deer. There were apples, pears, plums, grapes and more in the orchard. Other wildlife, like pheasants, blue jays and woodpeckers, as well as raccoons and squirrels, came to the orchard for food.

Dad was happy to let me go hunting by myself, but he wouldn't let me go with any of my friends. He figured that it was safer for one person to be out with a gun than it was for two people to be out together.

One day I noticed that the plum tree branches were pulled down so the tips touched the ground. I told Dad about it when I got home. He figured that a black bear must have been in the orchard and warned me not to go up there until someone got it. Mr. Ruckle shot the bear a few weeks later, but by then it had already killed several of his sheep.

When there weren't any bears around, I took my twenty-two and went hunting when I got home from school. There were lots of blue grouse up in the mountains and pheasants down in the fields too. Generally, I brought home a couple of blue grouse. In the evening the pheasants came in from the field and settled into the stumps and bracken where my house sits now. Sometimes Jim and I went down and got a pheasant or two.

☙ I enjoyed taking my dog, Bowser, pheasant hunting in the Fulford Valley. (circa 1948)

Fishing

About the same time that I was learning to hunt, Grannie took me to Fulford Harbour and taught me to rake herring. Traditionally, Indian herring rakes were made from bone needles, but ours was made of sharp bicycle spokes. As we dragged our rake through the schools of herring, some got stuck on the sharp spokes. We'd bring a bucketful of herring home and smoke them.

We threaded the herring on long sticks—in through the gills and out through the mouth. By the time we were done, the fish hung neatly in a row with their tails hanging down. Every morning for two or three days, we lit a small maple wood fire in Grannie's smokehouse and smoked the herring quite heavily so they'd be dry enough to store in her attic. Some evenings we toasted a few herring over the hot coals in the fire, just like they were marshmallows!

Clams

When I was about eight years old I helped Grannie and her family harvest clams. In the middle of September they set up camp out Fulford a ways, off what is now Isabella Point Road, where a stream flowed into the ocean. Once they had a few sacks full, they dried the clams so they would keep all year.

They dug a four by eight foot pit on the beach, filled it with about eight inches of rock and built a fire on top. When the rocks glowed red hot, they scraped away the ashes and laid seaweed on top. Oh, it would steam! The clams were placed on top of the seaweed and another layer of seaweed was piled on top of that. Grannie made grass mats that she put over everything to keep in the steam. About an hour later, they removed the mats and the seaweed to find that the shells were open.

Before the clams were totally cooked, they took them off the rocks, punched a hole through each of them and threaded them onto cedar bark. They made long strips—maybe half an inch wide and maybe ten feet long—from the inside bark of the cedar tree. The strings of clams were hung on a rack over a small fire. The fire was never very hot; it provided just enough smoke to keep the flies away. The early fall sun dried the clams a golden brown and the little bit of smoke kept them fresh. The clams dried this way for about five or six days before they were stored for the winter. Grannie hung hers in her attic rafters to keep them dry.

The dried clams lasted all winter. We just took them off the string and ate them. They were really good. I used to have them all the time.

Harvesting Rock Cod

When I was in my mid-seventies, my wife Molly and I found out the hard way that times had changed quite a bit from when Grannie and her family harvested all the seafood they needed from the ocean.

Molly and I collected crabs the smart way. I put a pitchfork underneath them, lifted them and put them into our bucket. We had found some good ones, so Molly had started walking home while I poked around a bit longer on the shore. When a chap came up behind me and asked what I was doing, I knew that Molly had our bucket of crabs. I told him the only sensible thing—that I was trying to get some rock cod.

The man, who turned out to be a conservation officer, accused me of looking for crabs, which I flatly denied. I was charged anyways and had to go to court in Duncan to face the judge.

The judge explained to the court that I had been charged for getting crabs with a pitchfork. I insisted that I was just spearing codfish with the pitchfork, which is perfectly allowable! The judge asked the man who charged me if I had any crabs in my possession when he saw me. This fella had to admit that I had no crabs. "Well," the judge asked, "Did you see him pick any up with the pitchfork?"

"No Sir," the officer admitted.

Just for fun, I said, "Your Honour, he hasn't any proof that I was getting crabs with the fork. I'd like you to dismiss the case."

"Case Dismissed!" the judge declared.

More Crab Troubles

Another time, we were walking home along the beach when we ran into a nice bunch of crabs. We ended up with eleven of them in our buckets—a fine feast for our big family. Molly was walking up the trail from the beach ahead of me when the fish warden came out to see her. We were allowed to have only four crabs each, so we were three over our limit. While the warden was counting the crabs in Molly's bucket, I was throwing the three extra ones away. By the time he looked in my bucket, we were OK. Otherwise, we would have had to pay a $40 fine. It would have been an expensive crab dinner!

Salmon, Trout and Herring

A salmon-spawning creek runs right through our family farm. When I was young, a large number of fish spawned there during the winter months. About January and February the creek was quite high and we got lots of trout. Sometimes we caught cutthroats that weighed up to four pounds and measured up to two feet long! If we wanted trout for supper, we could catch one or two just by throwing our line off the bridge.

The spring salmon came when the herring were spawning in February and March. Many a day I went to the bay at daylight and caught a couple salmon before school started. I sold them for 10 cents a pound. That was a great trade for me because I could buy a chocolate bar for 5 cents in those days.

Here I am with a prize catch of salmon that I caught from my rowboat in Fulford Harbour over a span of two hours. The largest one was twenty-six pounds, the next two were sixteen pounds, the last two were twelve and eight pounds. (circa 1940)

Dad didn't like it much, but in the summertime we took the rails off his fence, laid them across the creek and shoveled dirt in to make a dam. We raised the creek a couple of feet and used it for our swimming hole. We spent a lot of our time swimming in the creek.

When friends from Victoria came over for a swim, I liked to play a trick on them. I held onto our round galvanized wash tub and told one of the kids to get in. Once they got in, I encouraged them to start paddling around, as if they were in a little boat. There's just no way to float a galvanized wash tub like that. As soon as I let go, it tipped over. They landed upside down in the water every time!

Me, Bill Hill and my brother Jim in the creek. (circa 1920)

Gathering

Grannie introduced me to wild blackberry picking when I was young.

When she was young herself, Grannie collected berries in the fall, when there was lots of sugar in them. She ground them into a thick jam in the carved basin of a big boulder and patted the mixture into little cookies that she dried in the sun. When they were dry, she brought them in the house where they kept all winter long. She and her family ate the dry fruit cookies for dessert. She said they were good, but she never made them for me.

Berry picking was one of my least favourite activities, but I made the best of it because I was always glad to go out with Grannie. She had a big berry basket that she had made herself out of cedar bark. It had some kind of a crocheted or knitted strap that went around her neck and the basket hung on her chest so she had both hands free for picking.

She made one for me too. My basket was much smaller, but that didn't make the job any more enjoyable. I always tried to get it done faster by filling my basket half full of leaves. After I'd picked just enough berries to cover the leaves, I showed Grannie my little basket full of berries. She knew I was fooling, but she'd praise me and tell me what a good berry picker I was!

As I got older, I found the berry-picking job easier to take. I remember picking chummuk berries with Grannie. They started out green and smooth, but we didn't pick them until they got quite large and turned red. They were a little fuzzy and very sticky around the outside. I liked squeezing them until all the seeds squirted out all over the place. We call them gooseberries now, but considering how sticky they are, the Indian word for pitch, 'chummuk,' seems more appropriate.

Grannie showed me what plants were good to eat and what plants to avoid. In the spring, when the first leaves come out, new plant shoots are sweet and tender—and really good to eat. When the new salmonberry shoots—Grannie called them thaskies—were about a foot high, we broke them off, peeled the skin and ate them raw. We did the same with mukmuk, the new shoots off the button-berry bush. Grannie said that oregon grape shoots were healthy, kind of like a spring tonic to tone up the blood, so we ate those too. Even now, if I'm out in the woods in the spring and I see some light green leaves, I'll chew them up and swallow the juices.

Greybearded moss is another way nature provides nourishment. The plant grows high up on the bark of old growth trees and blows down during a snowstorm. When their other food is covered by snow, deer can survive on the moss. Second growth forest is too thick together for the moss to grow, so it's probably a good idea to preserve some old growth trees for the benefit of the animals.

Grannie used to chew the moss, swallow the juice and spit out the fibre. I don't know that you could ever get fat on it, but if there was so much snow on the ground that you couldn't get anything else, you could always eat the moss!

Clearing Land

The land all around my house was full of big stumps when I was young. Some of them had been there since the early years when Granddad Akerman first cleared the land. It was very difficult to remove them with horse and oxen in those days, so the stumps were often left to rot.

Dad and I used stumping powder shots to clear the stumps so that the land would be more usable. Stumping powder works well because it lifts the stumps out of the ground in pieces. Sometimes, when a big stump came only part way out of the ground, we had to rely on the horses to pull it out, just like in the old days.

I cleared a lot of land with my dad. Our little black spaniel, Carlos, was with us when we were clearing the land where the ball field is now, just behind the house. Carlos usually waited patiently beside us for the blast and then tore back to the site where he dug furiously in an attempt to find the source of the smoke.

One day I had put two big shots under a stump and when it was ready to go I lit the fuse. Dad and I stood back so we wouldn't get hit with the debris and waited for the blast.

Dad was the first to notice that Carlos wasn't around. I called him, but I guess he didn't hear me. An instant after the blast, the dog was tumbling through the air. He came down hard, but jumped up and ran into the house. Carlos lay down and waited until the next day to help us clear land.

I did a lot of farm work for Dad when I was living at home in the 1930s. That's how I contributed to the family. We had two horses, several cows, pigs, chickens, ducks, geese, guinea fowl and a herd of sheep.

I learned almost everything I know about sheep farming from Dad. Jim and I helped herd and shear the sheep from when we were quite young. As I got older, I rode one of the horses to bring the cattle in from pasture.

The animals weren't the only things on the farm that needed work: Dad was always planting something! We grew a lot of wheat, oats, potatoes and other crops. As I got a little older I drove the horses with the mower to cut the hay. After, I'd rake it, load the wagons with it and unload it into the barns.

We stored the hay in the loft so we could feed the horses and cows through the wintertime. The hay loft at the back of the barn went from the ground, right up to the rafters. Jim and I liked to climb up onto the rafters and jump down twenty feet or so into piles of loose hay.

It wasn't anything special at the time—just all-around farm work—but it was great experience and gave me lots of great memories.

Haying

In the old days farmers managed their hay crops a little differently than they do now. They plowed and reseeded their fields every six or seven years. The quality of their hay was much better than what I see on the fields these days, and there was much more of it too. Here's how they did it:

To start with, the farmers always made sure their fields were well drained. They dug ditches to drain away the water, so they could start working on their fields early in the spring, when other, non-drained areas were too wet. Then, they used some special field preparation and planting techniques.

The first year, after plowing the sod under, they disked and harrowed the soil in preparation for seeding. When the fields were smooth and level, they planted oats. They had a trick for determining when it was time to cut the oats for hay in the fall. Periodically, they would crush a seed head from their oat crop between their fingers. When milk came out of the seed head, it was time to harvest. Afterwards the farmers pastured the land with their animals.

The second spring, they plowed to bring the rotten sod back to the surface to make a good seedbed and then they harrowed in preparation for seeding. This time, along with the oats, they planted a mix of grass seeds and red top and elsa pink clover. The oats protected the grass from drying out in the summer. The clover does well for the first couple of years. By the time it dies out, there is a good crop of grass hay in the field. After harvesting that fall's hay crop, which was a mixture of oats and hay grass, the farmers didn't pasture their land. They were protecting the new grass that was growing in anticipation of a good hay crop the next year.

The third year, they cut good heavy crops of hay in July. By now, the grass had a good root base, so they pastured it again after the harvest.

For the next five or six years, the farmers continued harvesting in July and pasturing their fields until the spring. The seventh year, they started over with a new crop of oats in the spring.

Power of Positive Attitudes

One of my least favourite jobs was taking the horses to the blacksmith in Ganges. If we had the horses on the road, we had to shoe them so that their hooves wouldn't crack. The trip to Ganges was a long one with horses and wagon. It took two hours each way, with no music and no company. I wouldn't even pass any cars on the road!

Even though I didn't like the trip very much, I tried to keep it all in perspective. I had seen first-hand what a difference a positive attitude can have on life.

For a time, my Grandmother Akerman lived with us and my Grannie Gyves lived across the street. These two women could not have been more different, both in their upbringing and in their views on life. My grannie was always very positive and saw the best in life. My grandmother, on the other hand, always expected to see the worst and this perspective affected everything she did.

One sunny summer morning, when Grannie was over visiting, I overheard her say in a cheerful voice, "Isn't it a beautiful day, Mrs. Akerman?"

Grandmother obviously heard what she wanted to hear and didn't hesitate a moment before gloomily replying, "Yes, it looks likes it's going to rain."

It wasn't often that Grannie responded to Grandmother Akerman's doom and gloom, but one day she'd obviously had enough. When Grannie had asked Grandmother Akerman how she was doing and Grandmother had responded with her usual negative attitude, Grannie suggested: "Well, why don't you just go jump in the creek then?"

Farming

Every year a thrashing machine came through the valley and stopped at each of the farms, one after the other. About ten local farmers cooperated during thrashing season to thrash at each man's farm until they were all done. This helped get the job done quickly and cost the farmers less for the use of the machine than it would have if they had each worked alone. Sharing the work among many hands made it more enjoyable too.

At each farm, the farmer's wife made dinner for the work crew to show the couple's appreciation for the hard work that had been done that day. There was a competition among the farmers' wives to put on the best meal of the season. I guess it was prestige; they wanted the farmers to go home and tell their wives, "Mrs. So-and-So makes the best food I have ever eaten!" The wives always did their best to get a real nice dinner and they always tried to have it ready right when we came in from the field so we wouldn't be hungry. When we went out to thrash, we always knew we were going to get the best.

Unexpected Dinner Guests

The people who owned the last farm on our list weren't fussy about anything. This farmer and his wife didn't have any children and they didn't keep things in very good shape, the way some farmers do. Eight of us were out in the field thrashing that day while the lady cooked dinner for us. We weren't too sure what kind of dinner we were going to get, but when we were done we went in for dinner anyways.

The husband, who was a mechanic, stopped along the way to help one of the farmers fix his car. The rest of us were hanging out in the yard, where the farmer and his wife had their chickens running around.

The lady had the table all set, so she came out to the yard to let us know. "Dinner's all ready!" she called. "It'll be getting cold, so you better come in!"

We all trooped into the kitchen, only to find the chickens on the table picking at the roast! They had been running all over the place and nobody noticed that they had gone into the kitchen. "Oh my goodness!" the wife moaned.

Like an old pro, she went into action, flapping her big white apron up and down, side to side, shooing the birds outside. Feathers were flying, birds were squawking and our cook was yelling "shoo, shoo, shoo!" After our long day of thrashing, the crew and I watched in amazement and guarded our heads as the chickens flapped around the kitchen, banging into one another, the walls and the table in an effort to get back to the relative calm outside.

After no small effort, we got the chickens back out into the yard. We were gathered back in the dining room, wondering what would happen next, when the farmer's wife sighed, and said: "One thing I don't like is chickens on the table when I'm eating!" With that, she sat down at the table to eat. We had no choice but to sit down with her to eat what was left after the birds had taken their turn!

Thrifty

One of the farmers in our thrashing crew was Scottish. The Scots have a reputation for being tight with their money and he was that way too. When we got to his place, there was quite a crew—about seven or eight men—on the thrashing machine. It was always the same way at this man's farm. At eleven o'clock in the morning he came around to the crew with a big bucket of apples. "Lots of apples here! Apples for everybody! Help yourself!"

He forced apples on everybody so they wouldn't eat so much at dinner time! He did it so many times that he got himself a reputation for it. We would be working in the field when someone would notice the time and say, "He'll be along pretty soon with a bucket of apples!" Sure enough, we'd look over our shoulders and he'd be there.

Thrifty, Like His Dad

That Scottish farmer's son was just like his dad. He and I were the same age and I saw it all my life. He didn't like to spend his money. Even when we were young, he'd encourage me to buy candy and then stare at it until I gave him some. He did that with everybody and, over time, he got the same reputation as his dad.

I'm not positive that these stories are true, but I heard them from reliable sources and they're pretty funny, so I'm going to share them with you.

The farmer's son stayed with his dad for quite a few years, working on the farm. While he was living at home, he started to date a local girl and he went with her for about three years. His dad always discouraged him from getting married, probably because it would cost too much money. One day he came home and announced, "I'm gonna get married, Dad!"

"Oh no, you can't to that! You're much too young. You can't get married!"

"Oh yeah, Dad. I'm gonna get married. I got a bargain!"

"Oh yeah?" his dad said. His eyes sparkled. "You got a bargain? How's that?"

"She's a wee bit in the family way, Dad."

Because it was a two for one deal, the farmer thought that was a great deal! “Oh! That’s fine, then. You go get married, son!”

So he did. Even after he got married he was still pretty tight with the money. When a fella was that tight, Dad would say, “He’ll pinch a coin so tight the eagle will poop!”

Anyway, this guy was like that. When he and his wife got married, they drove his old Ford up-island to Nanaimo on their honeymoon. On the drive, his wife got caught short. He stopped at a garage so she could go to the washroom, but after she got there, she discovered that it was a pay toilet. She had to put a nickel in before the door to the toilet would open. Since she didn’t have one, she walked back out to the car and explained to her husband why she needed a nickel. He started to fish around in his pocket, but he stopped when he got an idea that might save him some money. “Are you sure it’s not just wind, dear?” he said.

Much later, I heard from a friend that this guy had found a unique way to save money on groceries. My friend was working with him one day when they stopped for lunch. They had brought their lunches to work with them and, as was customary, each peeked into the other’s lunch pail to see what they had brought to eat. When my friend looked into this guy’s box, he was surprised to see a pair of false teeth sitting right on top of all the food. “I didn’t know you had false teeth,” he said with surprise. When this guy admitted that he didn’t, my friend couldn’t help but to ask why the teeth were in the pail.

“Oh, I always take the wife’s false teeth when I leave for work,” he said. “I don’t want her eating between meals!”

☙ My dad would describe a very thrifty person by saying: "He'll pinch a coin so tight the eagle will poop!"

Piers Island

Many Salt Spring Islanders, including myself, played an interesting part in a piece of Canadian history through our work on Piers Island. This small island, which is located in the Satellite Channel between Swartz Bay and Salt Spring Island, attracted attention from across Canada in the 1930s when the government chose to locate a special temporary prison there.

Prison

The government built a prison on Piers Island for the Sons of Freedom sect of the Doukhobor religion. Doukhobors were pacifists that had come to Canada from Russia to avoid persecution for their religious beliefs. They lived happily in the Kootenay region of British Columbia for quite some time, until their beliefs began to clash with the expectations of the Canadian government.

In response to government authority and the financial effects of the Depression, some Doukhobors created a very strict sect called the Sons of Freedom. Members of the Sons of Freedom strongly resented government efforts to make them assimilate into Canadian culture. They were extremely upset about the government's insistence that they enroll their children in the public school system. The Sons of Freedom used civil disobedience to demonstrate their displeasure; this strategy was not only ineffective, it also created distrust and negative feelings among many Canadians.

The authorities also looked very negatively upon such displays. When several schools in their area were destroyed by arson, the Sons of Freedom were suspected immediately. Because there was no proof, no charges could be laid in regards to the arson, but hundreds of Sons of Freedom were later convicted for civil disobedience, which included the nude protests they staged in opposition to the government.

A special prison was needed to house these prisoners, so the government leased Piers Island from Bob Harvey and began constructing the facilities. Two compounds were built on the island—one to hold the men and another to hold the women—and they were separated by a double barbed wire fence. There were about twenty-six buildings in all, including dormitories, kitchens and clubhouses. Some of the buildings were more than one hundred feet long. A long dock was also built so that the *Cy Peck* ferry could access the island.

Working

Quite a few Salt Spring Islanders got jobs on Piers Island. Friends of mine were employed as builders, cooks and guards. The prisoners had a good place to live and they were treated very well for the three years of their prison term. The buildings were all clean and brand new. There were big wood burning heaters to keep the dormitories cosy and warm. Outside, they had large vegetable gardens and flower beds to tend. I heard from my friends that the prisoners said that they had never had it so good.

After their time was up, many of the Doukhobors refused to leave. It seems that they preferred life in their own island prison to what they had back in the Kootenays. When the first boat came to take them off the island, the guards had to herd them all down to the dock. As the boat landed, the former prisoners undressed—right at the dock! They were put in jail for undressing, so they probably thought that they might get put back in prison for stripping down again. Their tactic did not work.

Cleaning Up

The government's contract had stipulated that the government would forfeit anything that was left on the island at the end of their lease. The government left all of the facilities standing, so a few months after the prisoners left, the island's owner, Bob Harvey, set about cleaning up. He could have left the buildings there, but they wouldn't have been much good to anybody. Instead, Bob contracted the demolition to Tom Isherwood, who hired Gavin Reynolds and myself to help him tear down the buildings.

When we were taking the buildings apart, we found a lot of things stashed away in the floors and walls. Under the floor we found silverware and tools. Some light-fingered prisoners must have put things in the floorboards so that they could come back and get them sometime. I also found an interesting picture behind a wall. It was a picture of this chap plowing his garden up in the Kootenays. He was holding the handle and there were six women pulling his little plow! I'll bet those women were happier to get to the jail than anybody!

We spent more than three months pulling every nail out of each piece of lumber in those buildings. It was all number one lumber and sold for $10 per thousand feet. After everything was torn down, Bob put the island up for sale for $40,000.00.

9

Ferries

FERRIES HAVE GIVEN SALT SPRING ISLANDERS A SENSE OF FREEDOM and frustration that most Canadians never get to experience. Over the course of my life, I have seen the ferry service evolve from a three-hour adventure to a regularly scheduled thirty-five minute ride. I have also had the opportunity to learn about and get to know some of the characters involved with providing this unique island experience.

Waiting in the ferry line at Fulford Harbour. (1932)

ꞶꞶ New arrivals at Fulford Harbour. (1932)

SS Iroquois

When it began serving the Gulf Islands in 1901, the *SS Iroquois* was one of the first Canadian Pacific Railway (CPR) boats to travel around the Gulf Islands picking up produce, taking it to Victoria, and delivering groceries and mail. It was a good thing for the five hundred or so settlers on Salt Spring because it simplified their travel to Vancouver Island, where they bought and sold supplies. It was still not an easy trip, however. It took about three hours to get from Victoria Harbour to Fulford Harbour on the *Iroquois*.

On November 13, 1911, the *Iroquois* was in Sidney, being loaded with hay for the Gulf Islands. Its next stop was Fulford Harbour and the passengers waited patiently as the crew stacked several tonnes of hay up on the top deck.

About that time, it started to blow a big heavy South-East off Sidney. Grannie's brother and father and some friends had been canoeing from Cowichan to Sidney. They got about a mile from Sidney when the storm came up. It was blowing so hard that they pulled their canoes into the shore and built a fire. From the beach, they were alarmed to see the *Iroquois* pulling out into the water from Sidney, heading towards Fulford Harbour.

The *Iroquois* got out about a half a mile when the wind hit the hay up on the top deck. It was hit so hard that the entire boat turned over on its side. Wasting no time, the Indians grabbed their canoes and set out towards the boat. They paddled through the heavy swells and rescued a good number of passengers.

They were heading back into shore when Grannie's brother saw something that looked like a black mat floating on the water. They paddled over to it and saw that it was a mass of hair. When he reached into the water to grab it, he discovered a woman under the water. She was half-drowned, but they were able to revive her and bring her in to shore. She was a schoolteacher who was taking the CPR boat to Galiano Island where she worked.

In all, about twenty passengers and crew drowned. Later it was determined that the accident was caused because the ferry was overloaded.

That afternoon, before anyone on the island heard the news, Mr. Charles Appleby went into Bill McAfee's blacksmith shop and announced, "Something terrible happened today!" Mr. Appleby was an eccentric black man who lived just above Ganges.

Mr. McAfee humoured him by asking, "What happened?"

"Well," said Mr. Appleby, "the *Iroquois* sunk and lost some passengers." Mr. McAfee thought he was just talking, but that evening he got word that the *Iroquois* had sunk. No one can say for sure how Mr. Appleby knew before anyone else.

About a week later, the mailbag for the Gulf Islands washed up on the shore on Knapp Island, just off of Swartz Bay. Someone found it and the post office dried the mail and delivered it. I have a letter of my dad's that went down on the *Iroquois*. It is the letter from the government that appointed him justice of the peace for Salt Spring Island.

Hepburn's Ferry

Hepburn's Ferry, which started business in the early 1920s, was the first one to run between Fulford Harbour and Swartz Bay. It was a private enterprise owned by Mr. John Hepburn.

Mr. Hepburn had made a lot of money in the Klondike on the trail of 1898 and he invested it in the Victoria area. Around 1925, Mr. Hepburn financed the landing slip at Swartz Bay and he put in the road to Sidney. At one time, Mr. Hepburn owned a full block of buildings in Victoria.

I remember the carpenter, Charlie Urquhart, building Hepburn's Ferry on Fulford beach right in front of the stone church. The ferry was built in the shape of a scow and powered by a Fordson farm tractor. It had room for about four cars and made the trip in two hours.

There were several pulleys on the ferry's drive shaft so that, if there was a heavy head wind blowing and a Ford Model T car on board, Mr. Hepburn could hook up the car for some extra power. After getting permission from the car's owner, he would jack up the back wheel of the car and attach a belt from the model T's back wheel to the ferry's drive shaft and start the car.

Bea Hamilton was a writer who came to Salt Spring Island at the turn of the century and wrote for the *Sidney Review* and *The Driftwood*. The Hamilton and the Hepburn families were good friends. Bea wrote a song to tease her friend Mr. Hepburn, the man who owned the ferry. She played her ukulele and sang her lyrics to the tune of a popular vaudeville song, 'Mister Gallagher and Mister Shean.' We all enjoyed it! I think the words went something like this:

There was a funny man,
As funny as can be.
His name was Mr. Hepburn,
He was born in 1873.
To make himself a name,
As Noah did the same,
He built himself a scow
That put the ark to shame.

Oh Mr. Hepburn, Oh Mr. Hepburn,
He built himself a ferry so to speak
He built it for a song, It was broad as it was long
and a trip to Swartz Bay takes him near a week.

Oh Mr. Hepburn, Oh Mr. Hepburn,
From what we've seen, what we've seen
There sure was something funny in his bean.
His idears were all abunk
When he built that pile of junk.
Oh Absolutely, Mr. Hepburn!
The whole thing is a scream!

Hepburn's Inventions

While he was working on the ferry, Mr. Hepburn worked at a sideline. He had quite a few dairy cows and he used their milk to make cheese in big round blocks. The blocks were huge—so big that he made more cheese than he could sell. The cheese tasted good, but the times were pretty hard and nobody had the money to buy much of it.

After he had tried the car ferry for a year, Mr. Hepburn changed tactics and started up a foot passenger ferry. After that, he started farming full-time in the Beaver Point Road area, where a Christmas tree farm now stands.

He wanted to grow vegetables in the early spring and late fall, so he got the idea that he could extend the growing season by keeping the ground warm. He built a steam plant and hooked it up to a series of steel pipes that he buried under the ground throughout his big field. He powered up that steam plant, pushed the steam all through the pipes and warmed the ground. The vegetables didn't grow worth a darn, but he tried anyways. Mr. Hepburn was clearly a very inventive man.

Cy Peck

Back in the 1930s, I was down at Fulford when the *Cy Peck* ferry caught fire. It was a private ferry at that time: Salt Spring Lands, a real estate outfit in Ganges, and the government got together on this ferry so more people from Victoria would come buy land on Salt Spring. It was noontime and nobody was around at all when I saw the smoke. I ran down to the dock, yelling "Fire!", but I was all alone. The door leading to the fire was locked so I scrambled up the side of the boat with a hose. It was quite steep, but I got up there!

I could see that everything was burning down below me. The canvas on top of the lifeboat and the paint on the wheelhouse were burning. There was smoke everywhere. First, I got the hose and sprayed water on the paint. Then I sprayed the canvas. After I got that fire out, I tore the ropes off the canvas and I threw them in the water. They were blazing as they fell down into the water and they smoked pretty heavy after they hit, too!

By then somebody must have spotted the smoke and told Captain Maude. He came running down to the docks from his house, which was just a few hundred yards up the hill on Morningside Road. At first he couldn't figure out what was going on. I think he thought I was trying to burn up the ferry! I had to explain what had happened: I figured that somebody on the top deck threw his cigarette butt over the side when he was about to leave the ferry. Instead of going over the side, the cigarette flew back and landed on the canvas and started the fire. It's easy for the summer wind to do that. That boat would have gone up in flames for sure if the fire wasn't put out so quickly! A couple of weeks later, Captain Maude came by my house with a case of beer to thank me for saving the ferry!

Alaskan Prince

In the 1940s we had some big freighters coming in to Fulford Harbour. They docked at the government wharf, near where the ferries docked. One time, the *Alaskan Prince*, a freighter that delivered supplies and explosives to the mines up north, came in and just about caused some big trouble.

The skipper of the *Alaskan Prince* decided to dock at the ferry wharf, but since the *Cy Peck* was already docked, there wasn't enough room for the freighter. Although the big ship was coming in very slowly, it bumped into the ferry before it could stop and tore off quite a bit of the ferry's railing. At the time, the ferry's captain was down on the deck helping direct the cars.

When the big boat bumped them, the ferry captain said something sarcastic to the skipper of the *Alaskan Prince* about banging the ferry and reminded him where the government dock was located. The skipper of the *Alaskan*

Prince looked down on the ferry with a sneer. Judging by the way that he talked, it seemed likely that he had enjoyed a few drinks while he was out on the water that day. "Who's the skipper of this tub?" he demanded.

Captain Maude, who was a very dignified English gentleman, replied, "I am, Sir."

"Then get up on the bridge where you belong!" the skipper hollered. He turned and walked back to the bridge. He reversed the *Alaskan Prince* out of the ferry docks and managed to get it docked at the government wharf, where it should have been docked the first time.

Later that day I walked down to the wharf to take a look at the *Alaskan Prince*. Inside, I saw hundreds of cases of dynamite. They were sitting in the front hold of the ship—right behind a stack of boxes of detonation caps! The part of the freighter that hit the ferry was full of dynamite that, if the boats had hit with more force, would have exploded in an instant! Not many people realize how close we came to a disaster at Fulford Harbour that day.

10

Logging

I KNEW MY DAD WANTED ME TO GO BACK TO SCHOOL after grade eight, but I couldn't imagine sitting in a classroom all day. I'd had my first taste of a regular paycheque on the prairies and I wanted more.

Mike Lumovitch

The first thing I did after getting home from the harvest was to see Mr. Mike Lumovitch about a job. Logging with Mr. Lumovitch in the Cusheon Lake/Blackburn Lake area that year, I learned a lot of things that I wouldn't have learned in school. I learned how to use an axe without cutting myself, how to fall a tree without hurting myself and, most importantly, when I was standing in the wrong place.

Big Lumber

We logged big timber in those days. They're taking out little second growth now, but we had first growth. The logs were six feet through and a lot of them were over one hundred feet tall before we bucked them to thirty-two feet. Some of those logs had five thousand board feet in them.

There were so many big logs around that they weren't worth very much. Now they calculate board feet a little differently than they did back then, but in 2003, one thousand board feet of two-inch by four-inch softwood lumber sold for US$299.50. In 2005 our provincial government estimated that prices for spruce, pine and fir would reach US$319.00 per thousand board feet. Back in the early 1930s, Mr. Lumovitch got $8 for every thousand board feet of wood he transported to the water at Ganges.

Even then, $8 per thousand board feet didn't provide very much money for all the work involved, so Mr. Lumovitch couldn't afford to pay very much for wages. There should have been about five or six of us working on the operation, but he could only afford to hire three of us. Each of us had to do two or three different jobs. The donkey puncher operated the machine, the man out in the bush hooked up the logs and I had a few different jobs. I gave the signals, unhooked the logs, cut wood for the donkey and did whatever else needed to be done at the time.

My first day in the bush, Mr. Lumovitch asked me to take the strawline up the hill and put it through the blocks. While I was on my way, he yelled, "Hurry up! Take short cuts with long steps!" I learned pretty fast that I couldn't dawdle on this job.

When we started a new setting, two of us worked together to fall the trees. We used axes and those big crosscut saws. Sometimes trees that were four or five feet through were too tough to cut with our saws, so we used springboards to get us about three feet off the ground, up to where the wood was not so tough and so thick.

ଓ Leon King and a fellow logger standing on springboards to cut a tree with a crosscut saw. (circa 1914)

The springboard was about six inches wide by five feet long and had a steel tip on the end. This steel tip anchored the springboard into a notch we made in the tree. Once our springboards were anchored, we scrambled up, grabbed hold of the cross saw and started dragging it through the tree, first in my direction, then in his and back again. We were careful to keep the saw straight so it wouldn't bind in the tree.

It was tough to be up on a springboard, sawing back and forth and sweating away in hot weather. Boy! That was tough! While we were sawing away, those darn black flies would get on our backs and start chewing us up, but we couldn't stop sawing. We couldn't stop for anything because if one guy stopped, he would throw the whole rhythm out for the other guy and the job would take far longer than it should.

Steam Donkey

Mr. Lumovitch had the island's first steam donkey, made by the Willamette Iron and Steel Works of Portland, Oregon. It rested on a sleigh that we built from huge fir timbers. A big boiler made steam that powered three winches: one for the mainline, one for the haul-back line and one for the strawline. We were always feeding firewood into the donkey to keep the boiler hot. And because the engine would explode if it ever ran dry, we always had to have lots of water nearby too.

After we had cut down two or three hundred trees, we set up the steam donkey to haul in all the logs. We used the steam donkey's winches to drag it to its new location. By attaching the mainline to a stable tree or stump that acted as an anchor, and going ahead on the mainline, the winch pulled the sleigh along towards the anchor. We continued with that process until the steam donkey was properly positioned.

Often, the donkey puncher and the man in the bush could not see each other and, because the machine was so loud, they couldn't hear each other either. One of my jobs was to relay signals between the two men so that they could move the logs quickly without anyone getting hurt. I usually stood on a high knoll or stump, close to the machine, where I could see the donkey puncher and the fella in the woods. The woodsman hooked the log onto the mainline and gave me a signal that it was all right for the steam donkey to go ahead. I passed that signal to the donkey puncher and he started the winch to pull the log in to the cold deck.

Usually we gave hand signals to indicate it was time to start the winch, but sometimes we were too far apart to see one another. In those cases we strung a jerk wire from my position to a whistle on the donkey sleigh. When I pulled the wire, the whistle blew to signal the donkey puncher.

Once we had winched in all the logs from the setting, the cold deck was about thirty feet high. We used the steam donkey to load the logs onto our truck for the drive to the water.

I got paid 25 cents an hour for the hours I worked, which usually gave me $2 at the end of the day. Logging was dangerous work and it wasn't worth much back then. Lots of people got killed in the early days. We lost at least ten men from Salt Spring to logging since it started back at the turn of the century. Many more men got seriously hurt.

Donkey Maintenance

The old steam donkeys required regular maintenance and the owner and his crew had to keep them in good shape. After moving the sleigh around from setting to setting, the timbers that it rested on became worn. The machinery itself also showed the strain of the heavy work it did each day and its parts required maintenance.

Every once in a while we had to build a new sleigh for the donkey and replace the bearings on the cable drums. Normally this had to be done once every twenty years or so, but it needed to be done more often if the sleigh wasn't well maintained.

To build a new sleigh for the donkey, we started by falling two huge trees that were about four feet through so they landed side-by-side and fairly close to one another. We cut these logs into forty foot lengths, stripped their bark and, using an axe, shaped them to act as rails on the sleigh. Cross pieces held the rails steady while we used a hand auger to bore holes through the logs. We hammered iron rods through the holes and bolted it all together.

We moved the steam donkey beside the new sleigh using the winches. We undid all the old bolts so that the machine was moveable. Then, by hooking the mainline up to an anchor, just as we would do to move the sleigh to a new setting, we slid the machine bit by bit onto our new sleigh and bolted it all down again. This was a slow and careful process because the machine weighed more than several tonnes. Even though we always brought in an extra man to help put the donkey on a new sleigh, it generally took about two weeks to build the new sleigh, move the donkey, and have the whole setup ready to go.

New Bearings

One time Mr. Dave Maxwell was the donkey puncher, also known as the steam engineer. He was my friend Steven's dad and had gone to school with my father. Mr. Maxwell was in charge of replacing the worn bearings on the cable drums. Every once in a while the bearings got so worn that they weren't round anymore; when they got to be an oblong shape, the winches wouldn't run smoothly. The old bearings had to be taken out with a hammer and chisel before they could be replaced with new ones that were made out of babbitt.

Babbitt is a very hard substance that was used for low friction bearings before ball bearings were invented. It is a metal alloy made of tin, antimony, copper and often lead. To make new bearings, babbitt must be heated until it forms a liquid-like substance that can be poured. Babbitt can't be run in the rain, though, because if hot babbitt touches anything wet, it will explode.

Mr. Maxwell and I went up to the site one morning to run the new bearings on Mr. Lumovitch's machine. Once we had removed the old bearings, Mr. Maxwell was ready to pour the babbitt. It started to rain a little bit, though, so we went home to wait for better conditions. It quit raining later that day and, by the next morning, everything was dry. Or at least it looked dry. It might have rained again some time in the night because water got down into the bottom of the shaft somehow. Whatever happened, we didn't notice until it was too late.

Running the Babbitt

Mr. Maxwell got his fire going so strong that the coals were red hot. He put the babbitt in a big iron ladle and held it in the fire for quite a long time until it started to melt. He said that as soon as the babbitt turned blue it would be hot enough to pour. We watched it melt and turn into a kind of fluid. When the babbitt turned real good and blue, Mr. Maxwell carried the big iron ladle full of babbitt onto the sleigh.

I was standing alongside him when he started to pour. I saw the steam begin to come up. I didn't even have time to think that something might be wrong—the steam just came up a little bit and then she exploded. She threw babbitt everywhere—all over the roof of the donkey, all over everything. The sound rang in my ears like somebody let off a charge of dynamite in my face.

Without thinking, I jumped off the sled, down into the bush. When I came to my senses, I crawled out of the brush and scrambled up onto the sleigh to see how Mr. Maxwell was doing. He was standing dead still, holding the iron ladle. When I got right beside him, he didn't say a word. All I could think to ask was, "What are you still holding that ladle for?"

"Oh you're there," he said. "I didn't know where you were." I could see that the hot babbitt had exploded right in his face and had turned like birdshot. Mr. Maxwell stayed right where he was through it all—unbelievably, he was still holding the ladle. "If I dropped the ladle," he said, "it might have fallen on you and it would have burned."

He told me to put the ladle down somewhere safe, which I did quickly while telling him that I was going to take him down to see the doctor. I gently held his arm and led him down off the steam donkey. The walk to the road, through thick brush, over fallen trees and around big stumps, took longer than ever before.

I drove him down to see Dr. Lawson as fast and as smoothly as I could on those old roads in my Model T Ford. The doctor picked as much babbitt as he could out of Mr. Maxwell's eyes.

I saw Mr. Maxwell every day he was in the hospital. He had big bandages wrapped around his eyes, so I couldn't see how bad things looked and, of course, Mr. Maxwell couldn't see a thing. The doctor said the bandages needed to stay on Mr. Maxwell's eyes for about ten days, so he had to wait, not knowing if he had lost his sight in the accident. Fortunately, Mr. Maxwell could see a bit when the doctor first took off the bandages and he gradually got better after that.

Widening Cranberry Road

After our first experience putting in the babbitt bearings, we moved the steam donkey into the Cranberry. In the early days there was a marsh near where Cranberry Road is now. There were wild cranberries in there, so the old-timers called the area Cranberry Marsh. We slowly moved our steam donkey up through fields thick with sharp blackberry bushes and eventually hit Cranberry Road.

Because it was much easier to move the steam donkey on the main road than it was to move it through the brush, Mr. Lumovitch made a deal with the road people. They let him take his machine up the road if he would take some stumps off the corners to widen the road.

While we were pulling the stumps, Mr. Tweedhope, the provincial policeman, stopped to ask what we were doing. When we explained why we were pulling the stumps off the corners, he laughed. “Won’t that be handy for you young fellas! When you go up there to the bootleggers to drink wine, you won’t be runnin’ off the road comin’ home!”

Mr. Tweedhope had us figured out. We never had a liquor store here on Salt Spring in those days. To buy liquor legally, we had to go to Victoria. Since that was too far for anyone to go for a jug of wine, we bought it from bootleggers. My friends and I often went up to the Cranberry for a jug of wine or cider from the bootlegger. Bootleggers made wine and cider that was darn good! We had some really good parties with it!

Not all of the policemen were as quick to joke about the bootlegger as Mr. Tweedhope was. The police were in a tight spot when it came to the bootlegger and his wine. It was illegal to buy from the bootlegger, but with no liquor store on the island, the locals had no other option. Fortunately the police often turned a blind eye to those of us who travelled up to the Cranberry on a regular basis.

A Swede who had a tough time speaking English was working with us up at the Cranberry setting. One Friday while our logging crew was having lunch, we got to talking about getting some demi-johns of wine from the bootlegger. "Oh, my goodness!" the Swede said. "I forgot my yug!"

"What did you say, John?" I said.

"I forgot my yug."

"What's that? What's a yug?"

"You know I can't say yemiyon, Bob," he said. "So I gotta say yug!"

Christmas Trees

Christmas trees have been a popular custom in Canada for some time. In the thirties, when money was so hard to come by, loggers started looking for new ways to earn money from the land that had already been logged. In comparison to the huge first growth timber that we had been logging, small Christmas trees could be grown, cut and transported quickly. Salt Spring Island loggers, including myself, were keen to get into the Christmas tree market. I started out harvesting Christmas trees with Mike Lumovitch in the early thirties and continued in the business until the 1960s, when I passed it on to my eldest son.

Ladysmith

In 1932, Mike Lumovitch got an order for one hundred thousand Christmas trees from the Washington Christmas Tree Association of Seattle.

After he got permission to cut them on timberland property just north of Ladysmith, he rounded up twenty-six young fellas from Salt Spring and rented six or seven rooms in an old rooming house in Ladysmith. We called the middle-aged lady who looked after the place 'Granny' because she hated the nickname so much.

For better or for worse, I was nominated our room's cook. We all chipped in and I bought some stew beef for 10 cents a pound. With some potatoes, onions and carrots, I made a large pot of stew that the fellas could warm up when they got hungry. I made them macaroni and cheese every once in a while, for a treat. After all that effort, I was surprised that they still spent their own money on sandwiches from the restaurant!

We started cutting trees the first of November, 1932. We dragged them out to a road, picked them up with a truck and hauled them to the railroad landing where we tied them in bundles and loaded them in railroad cars to be hauled back to the USA. My job was to grade the trees into lots: fancy and standard. By the first of December, we had them loaded into twenty-six boxcars ready for shipment.

We made a lot of good friends while we were in Ladysmith. We met young people at the dances up the hill in a spot that the local people called Finn Town. We got into a few friendly fights with the local boys, but nothing very serious. For some reason, they didn't like us dancing with the local girls. The girls didn't seem to mind at all—they even asked us to walk them home!

I was interested in basketball at the time, so I used to go down and watch the Ladysmith teams play. They had a good Senior B team. One night, I told their coach that Salt Spring had a team and we could give them a good game. He thought I was joking and accepted my offer to bring the team up the next Saturday and commented that at least we would be good practice for his team. I never told him that we had won the Vancouver Island championship the year before! He didn't look so confident when we beat the socks off his team!

North Vancouver

The next year the Washington Christmas Tree Association asked me to go to the mainland to sort, cut and grade trees. They had a carload of trees to take out in North Vancouver, four carloads in the Fraser Valley and a carload on Scott Road in Surrey. I picked up Ed Reynolds, a young fella from Salt Spring who had worked with me in Ladysmith, and went over to the mainland. We didn't know where we were going to stay, but since we had some blankets in my 1927 Model T Ford, we were not too worried.

When we found the area we were to cut, just off Scott Road, we saw an old farm nearby. The farmer, Mr. Cromie, was a bachelor. He had a room that he wanted to rent for $5 for the month. That would have been a little steep for just a room, but it was a good deal for us because he gave us the use of the kitchen too.

The next day we had breakfast in the farmhouse, crossed the road from the farm to our work site and started cutting trees. Our lot was about twenty acres of fairly level ground with a good logging road through it. Logging work didn't get any easier than that! I helped Ed cut for a few days before I had to grade the other four loads of trees in the valley.

I took the ferry across to North Vancouver to a place called the British Properties. At that time, there were no houses in there—just Christmas trees. I graded until dark in the cold rain and then caught a ferry back to Vancouver.

I was so wet and cold that I decided to stay in town that night rather than drive back to the farmhouse. I dried out a little while having a 30 cent meal at a little diner called the White Lunch before taking a walk down Cordova Street.

I spotted an old rooming house that had rooms for 50 cents a night. The owner showed me to room that was a little worn, but clean. I was glad to take it. I laid my clothes out to dry and went right to bed.

Early the next morning I went back to the White Lunch for some breakfast. I explained to a young grey-haired lady who was looking after the cash that I was going back to work at the British Properties for a couple of days and needed some food to take with me. She made some lunches for me and I was all set.

When I got back to Vancouver a few days later, I went back to the boarding house and ate my meals at the White Lunch. The grey-haired lady at the cash was very nice and easy to talk to, so we always chatted when I went there.

Mr. Cromie's Housekeeper

While I was away, the farmer we rented a room from had put an ad in the paper for a housekeeper. He was excited when he got a phone call from a lady who said she would be over from West Vancouver the next day.

When my partner and I got home from work that day, she had already arrived. Her clothes appeared to be quite expensive, but they had seen better days and she looked just as tired. She stayed in her room during the day, but took off in the evening and was out until after midnight. She never did any housework.

One night, Mr. Cromie got fed up and locked her out. We woke up some time around midnight to the sound of her banging on the door, but since it wasn't any of our business, we went back to sleep.

The farmer found her sleeping in her car the next morning when he went out to milk the cows. He ran back to the house to let us know what he had found and warned us not to unlock the door to the house for her. He went back to the barn to do his chores while we started cooking our breakfast.

We hadn't finished our eggs when she started to pound on the door. I repeated Mr. Cromie's instructions and told her that I wouldn't open the door.

She wasn't as concerned about that as I would have thought, but asked me to get something for her out of her room. I grabbed the bottle full of white powder that she had described and handed it to her out the kitchen window. She seemed satisfied and was gone by the time we got home from work that night. We found out later that she was on drugs, which was probably the cause of all her problems.

A few years later, my cousin from Vancouver, Jim Parsons, came to Salt Spring for a visit. He was the son of Dad's sister Tilly. Jim was a deep sea captain who had travelled the world. I happened to mention that I had worked around Vancouver in the early 1930s and used to have breakfast at the White Lunch Cafe on Hastings Street. He told me that his sister Mattie worked there as a cashier in the 1930s. I might have recognized her, he said, by her grey hair. No doubt, I was talking with my first cousin without even knowing who she was!

Salt Spring Island

In 1934 I started wholesaling Christmas trees from Salt Spring. I supplied Art Knapp, who later had the Art Knapp nurseries in the Fraser Valley. I also supplied the Boy Scouts and the Boys Clubs in Victoria, among other businesses. My largest shipment was fifteen thousand trees to the USA. They were all cut on Salt Spring.

I harvested Christmas trees for almost three decades until my son Ted took over around 1960. He has supplied trees to Vancouver and Victoria ever since.

☙ Christmas trees in front of our house on Fulford-Ganges Road. (circa 1953)

Nanaimo Duncan Utilities

I worked logging on and off until 1934, when I started to work with the Nanaimo Duncan Utilities. Ronnie Lee and I were up north of Vesuvius Bay cutting piling for wharves when Mr. McDonald and Mr. Stevenson from the Nanaimo

Duncan Utilities came to the island. The company was planning to bring electric power to Salt Spring. We were working close to the beach when they came by looking for a good place to bring in the cable from Vancouver Island.

When we showed them an old trail in the bush that they thought was a good start, they asked us to slash the right of way so they could put the line through from Vesuvius across to Fulford.

Falling Danger Trees

Several other fallers worked on the smaller trees, but Ronnie and I got the job to fall the danger trees along the right of way. There was a lot of old growth—some trees were more than one hundred feet high—leaning over the highway. If one of those trees fell into the road, it would pull down the poles and all their wires as it went.

There was some skill involved with falling danger trees. We climbed as high up the tree as we could and attached a cable around the trunk. Back on the ground, we pulled the cable straight back into the bush, away from the road, and attached it to the trunk of a solid tree with a shackle. As we sawed the tree, we watched for the magic moment when the undercut started to lift. That was our sign to get out of there fast! As the trunk cracked, the cable pulled tight and the tree swung away from the road. I learned that trick when I was falling with Mike Lumovitch.

Once we removed the danger trees, the area had to be prepared for the hydro poles. Another gang of men came in behind us and determined where the poles would be placed. Each pole was set five feet down in the ground. Where possible, they dug the hole by hand; otherwise, they marked the spot and we came back later to blast the rock with dynamite. Blasting wasn't as easy as it sounds.

Blasting Dynamite

We had to hand drill holes in the solid rock before we could put in the dynamite. We pounded steel drills, which were about an inch thick, into the rock with eight pound sledgehammers. Sometimes one guy held the drill while two guys pounded it. One guy would hit—bang! As he was lifting his hammer again, the other guy would hit—bang! After each hit, the drill holder turned the drill. Turn it and hit it, turn it and hit it, turn it and hit it. Otherwise, the drill would go straight down and get stuck.

Once we had turned the drill completely so that it made a round hole, we put water down the hole. As we pounded and turned the drill, rock chipped into the water and mudded up like soft cement. We used a little tool that we called a spoon to collect the 'mud up,' and then we started again—sometimes with the same drill and other times with a longer one.

It was important to keep our tools sharp and I often worked on them in our little Hydro shop in the back of McAfee's Blacksmith Shop in Ganges. Sometimes the blacksmith called me to give him a hand. After he heated the iron and pounded it until it was ready to cut, he asked me to strike the drill. He'd be holding this darn thing and I'd be scared of hitting him on the hand or the wrist. "Don't be scared," he assured me. "If you ever miss the drill and hit the guy who's holding it, just blame him for moving the drill!"

We had drills of various lengths and widths to get down to the proper depth for the dynamite. We could start a hole with any length of drill we wanted, but it was smart to use one of the wider ones first. The longer drills had to be a shade smaller than what you started with to make sure they didn't get stuck. Our longest drill was about eight feet long. It was a big job to drill those holes by hand.

If the rock was sandstone, the work went pretty fast. But if the rock was granite, it took a long while to drill the hole. It took pretty well an entire day of swinging an eight pound sledge to drill a five foot deep hole in really hard granite. It wasn't as bad as it sounds, but we still preferred sandstone to granite!

One time, when four of us were all working on a ridge that had a similar class of stone throughout, we had a competition. My partner, Ronnie Lee, and I competed against two other drillers: Ray Morris and Dave 'Blackhawk' McKay. Dave, who used to play professional hockey for the Chicago Blackhawks, became an engineer for Hydro after he left sports. He couldn't stand working at a desk all day, so sometimes he came out and worked with us. After a hard fought competition, Ronnie and I won by drilling four holes for a total of about twenty-one feet in one day.

Once we had dug the hole to the depth we wanted it, we put in the explosive and blasted away. There was some skill involved with using just the right amount of dynamite to get a hole that was consistently sixteen inches wide all the way down five feet. If we put in too much powder, it would blast a hole in the shape of an ice cream cone; it would be too wide at the top and too narrow at the bottom.

Sometimes we got so accustomed to 'doing caps' that we got kind of careless. Those explosives are nothing to fool around with; they're full of nitroglycerin and a hard knock will let them go. Fortunately we didn't have any trouble.

Ronnie and I cut the danger trees and blasted rock for the main hydro line for almost six months before turning to the side lines that had to be prepared all over the island. In all, I spent about ten years with the Nanaimo Duncan Utilities, preparing the way for the lines that brought power all over the island.

11

The Ladies at Harbour House

SALT SPRING HAS ALWAYS BEEN SOMETHING OF A RESORT TOWN. When I was a young man, it was common for some companies in Vancouver to send their secretaries over to Harbour House for a summer holiday. These ladies always wanted somewhere to go and something to do while they were here and they always asked, "What can we do in a place like this?" Luckily for me and my friends, our buddy, Fred Morris, was dating the daughter of the chap that ran the Harbour House. Through him, we often got the opportunity to entertain the ladies from out of town.

Cusheon Lake Picnics

We didn't have much to entertain them with, but we made the best of what we had! If there was a dance at the Harbour House, we took them there. Other times, we took them down to Cusheon Lake where we had a wiener roast and went swimming.

Because they wanted the ladies to have so much fun that they would come again the next year, the Harbour House supplied us with wieners and buns for our picnic. The ladies, on the other hand, always wanted us to get beer!

As much as we would have liked to, we couldn't offer them any because we didn't have a liquor store on the island. I'd say, "Oh, we don't drink beer here. We drink loganberry wine and cider." They always thought that sounded good, so we'd go up to the bootlegger in the Cranberry and get ourselves a gallon of cider and a gallon of loganberry wine. We'd take our drinks and picnic supplies down to Cusheon Lake and have a grand time.

Most of the ladies teased us about drinking wine and cider. They'd say, "All you drink is apple juice!" By the time they figured out that the cider was quite strong, it was too late. After about three glasses, our group of ladies was a different bunch altogether!

Skinny-Dipping

When it was dark, they would all decide to go swimming. Each time, the ladies remembered that they didn't have their swimming suits with them only after they'd reached the water's edge. No problem! They got a good kick out of skinny-dipping off the dock in the moonlight. By the time they got back, Fred and the rest of us had the fire going and sticks ready for the wieners.

The ladies had a really good time with us and we always got them home safely. Fred's girlfriend looked after them back at the Harbour House.

A new bunch came every week throughout the summer. Each time, we'd say, "Sure! We'll do it again!" Those ladies must have had good times because Harbour House always had another crowd the next year.

Meeting Molly Morrison

Harbour House hosted dances in their ballroom every Saturday night and my friends and I went regularly. One night I noticed a couple of new girls—twin sisters. Before the evening was over, I managed to sit down and have quite a long talk with them. I learned that those twin sisters, Betty and Molly Morrison, had come from Vancouver to visit their dad who was building a summer home on Scott Road, outside of Ganges. Since they were staying with him for a couple weeks, my friends and I offered to show them around the island. After that, my cousin, Mac Mouat, and I took Betty and Molly out whenever they were around.

Molly was a very fine person and I could tell that right away. We liked a lot of the same things. She liked gardening and sports of every kind. She played softball all her life, but she was also a star track and field athlete in her day. When she was in high school in West Vancouver, she was a champion high jumper and she was good at the one hundred yards too. We got along very well together and I was always happy to see her.

The Morrison sisters came back again the following summer and Mac and I took them out some more. Eventually Molly decided to move here for good. I was thrilled about that decision because it meant that I got to see her more often.

ଔ Molly Morrison, the year I met her. That's her dad's cabin on Scott Road in the background. (circa 1936)

My sister Tilly, who was a registered nurse at Lady Minto Hospital, had heard that they were looking to hire a cook. Molly was interested in the job. Tilly worked six twelve hour shifts each week for $40 a month and she warned Molly that the job wouldn't be an easy one. Molly was never one to shy away from hard work and there weren't many jobs to choose from, so she thought she'd give it a try. The hospital hired her as the Head Cook, which we thought was kind of funny because she was the ONLY cook!

Molly worked from sunup until sundown in the kitchen. She started her day at six o'clock in the morning because the old iron stove took so long to warm up. Very often, she had a hard time even getting the fire started because the wood they gave her was so wet. By the time she got the breakfast made and the dishes done, it was time to start on lunch. So she'd start lunch and by the time she got everything clean again, it was time to get started with dinner. Lady Minto's fifteen rooms were full most of the time, so there were lots of meals to cook.

Monday to Saturday, she worked from six o'clock in the morning until seven o'clock at night. Sundays she worked from sunup until two o'clock in the afternoon. The rest of Sunday was her 'weekend.' She got paid $20 each month for her efforts. Molly worked at the hospital for over a year while I worked for Mr. Kellogg at his place on Bruce Mountain.

Molly and me. (circa 1937)

☙ This is a favourite picture of Molly (standing) and her twin sister Betty, taken long before I met them. (circa 1924)

12

One Last Talk with Grannie

I STAYED CLOSE WITH MY INDIAN GRANDMOTHER and I visited her often. On one of my visits, when I imagine she was close to one hundred, she didn't seem her usual happy self. She wasn't feeling well and I could tell that something was really bothering her, so I suggested that I take her to the hospital in Ganges. She didn't seem to think it would help at all, but I insisted. On the drive there she was unusually quiet despite my attempts to make conversation. Before I left the hospital, I assured her that I would come and take her home as soon as she was feeling better.

Grannie turned to me and took both of my hands into hers. She said quietly, "Bob, last night I heard the owl call my name—three times."

With those words, I could see her in her little white house more than twenty years earlier, carefully putting the duck feathers in the wooden box by the fireplace. I could recall her nervousness when, during one of my visits, an owl landed in the old apple tree just outside her house and started to hoot. "Hurry, Bob!" she urged. "Get some feathers out of the box and throw them on the fire!" She explained that we wanted the smoke to scare the owl away because "if it hoots too long, someone we know will die."

As a child, I sensed the urgency of her words and knew she was very serious when she told me, "When you hear the owl call your name, you won't have long to live. The Indians have believed this for generations."

While she was in the hospital at Ganges, I visited her as often as I could. I saw that she was getting lower all the time. One day she was quite low and the nurse cautioned me: "I don't know if she'll even know you now. She hasn't spoken for quite a while."

Grannie's Wolf Spirit

When I went in, Grannie was lying down with her eyes closed. I talked to her gently and, when she heard me, she reached her hand towards me. I held her hand and continued to talk. After a while, I felt soft vibrations in my hand. I noticed her hand was trembling too, but I couldn't figure out what was going on.

After we held hands for maybe two or three minutes, Grannie opened her eyes and started to talk. Gradually she became more aware and sat up in bed. We had a wonderful talk; it was very much like the conversations we had before she became ill. The nurse came in the room to check on Grannie and stopped in her tracks. "My goodness, Mrs. Gyves!" she said in amazement. "This is the first time you've been sitting up for several days."

Grannie and I talked just like old times, holding hands the entire time, and I was happy to think that she was going to be fine. After a while, it was time for me to leave, so I said goodbye and told her I'd be back again soon for another visit. I hadn't been home more than a couple of hours when the nurse phoned to tell me that Grannie had passed away.

Special Powers

I think Grannie must have been taking some power from me so we could talk one last time. I've never heard of anyone else transferring power like that, but I'm convinced that she used the power she gained from the wolf spirit that visited her when she was a young girl.

I had never seen her use her special powers before, but it was clear to me that night that she could do things that other people couldn't do. I have often wondered why she kept such powers secret. I feel very fortunate that she was able to break through whatever held her back the rest of her life so that we could have one last talk together.

13
Family

MOLLY AND I WENT TOGETHER FOR ABOUT THREE YEARS before we decided to get married. We started building our house in 1938 and got married the following year.

The Happy Couple

We had our marriage ceremony in the little stone church here in Fulford. Quite a few of our friends and relations were there. I took two or three days off work for our honeymoon. We borrowed my brother's 1936 Chevrolet and drove to Victoria to buy some furniture.

Not long after we got married, Molly cooked one of her first meals under some trees down at the beach. We had collected a big bucket of clams and she had cleaned them and put them into a Rogers' Maple Syrup can with some water. After hammering the lid tightly onto the can, she set it on top of the fire to boil. When the water heated, the pressure inside the can blew the lid right off! We were stunned by the noise—and surprised when we looked up to see our clam dinner hanging from the tree branches above us!

Molly and me on July 7, 1939, our wedding day. We borrowed my brother Jim's 1936 Chevrolet coupe for our honeymoon.

The Kelloggs' Farm

The year after we got married we lived at the Kelloggs' farm. They lived in Illinois, but had bought a big property near Musgrave Landing as a holiday spot. The Kelloggs knew they'd be away from Salt Spring for a while, so they asked Molly and I to take care of their place after we got married. Our house wasn't ready yet and it was a good opportunity for us. We jumped at the chance.

Mr. Kellogg paid us $60 a month to live at their house and do all of the farm work. They had a cow and a horse and some chickens to tend, but it was the other work that took up most of our time. It was an old farm, so a lot of the fence lines needed to be fixed and some big flower gardens needed to be tended. Molly and I were busy all the time, but it worked out well. Throughout the year that we lived at the Kelloggs', we spent the weekends working on our house.

ʚ The following excerpts are from courtship letters written by Molly's sister, Peggy Morrison, to her husband-to-be, Les Bryan, an electrician doing maintenance work on airplanes for Aviation Electric in Vancouver. These excerpts give a glimpse into life at the Kelloggs' farm and the general mood as we all prepared for World War Two:

July 7, 1939: Molly Morrison is no more! Molly and Bob were married this morning at 8:30am. She is now Mrs. R. Akerman. Imagine! I'm not sure if they spell it with a 'c' or a 'k'. Oh well! It was a quiet little wedding, but they had quite a sendoff. They both looked grand.

October 4, 1939: It's been a long time since I've mailed a letter to you. You know, I've been up in the hills for a whole week with Molly and Bob. I was just getting to be a good old hillbilly when I had to come home—which was today, about two hours ago.

I put five more pounds on. All the cream you could get down you, real nice thick cream and all the butter too. They make a lot of their own. Lovely fresh air—Molly and Bob have the cutest little fawn. Every morning we feed it with a bottle of milk. It comes right down to the house for it too.

Bob and I went fishing for a few nights. The first night I caught two big salmon. One was about 5 ½ pounds and the other was seven pounds. The next morning we got up at 6 o'clock and went fishing again. That time we caught two a bit smaller. Really, it's the swellest feeling to feel the first tug on the line. On Sunday morning we got up nice and early, had breakfast, then we all three of us piled into Bob's old truck and wee ee ee—over the mountain we went to see Bob's folks. They live in Fulford. It took one and a half hours to go over. Oh yes, Bob shot two grouse and one deer. On Sunday afternoon it rained like the old devil himself, just like it is now. It was getting dark, so Bob said we couldn't make it home at night over the slippery narrow roads. So there we stayed. Monday morning we were out before dawn. Bob was up at 4am and Molly and I were shortly afterwards. We were off over the mountain just as it was beginning to get light. More fun, eh?

February 28, 1940: Molly and Bob gave their notice and are coming back to Fulford to live. They'll be staying with the old folks till they get their own place ready to move in. That won't be till after May when the baby comes. Molly came over Tuesday, by boat, and Bob is coming sometime this week over the mountain with a load.

June 7, 1940: Molly and her baby and Bob were all down here last week for one day. Gee but the baby is cute. It's one month and one week old.

June 12, 1940: Bob has been very busy shearing sheep and so on. He works steady from 6am to about 8pm.

August 21, 1940: I went over to stay with Molly Saturday night and stayed till last night, Monday. Had a lovely time. Their baby Darlene is the cutest babe I've ever seen, she really is beautiful. She laughs and gurgles now and she's only three months old. Smart baby she is.

October 6, 1940: It's a beautiful day in Victoria today. All sunny and bright. Think I'll take a walk down and mail this and a few more letters I've written. Yes, they say baby Darlene is getting to be a big girl. I haven't been able to see the little darling for some time now.

This Friday all the Scottish left. 1,000 of them. All the Salt Spring Island boys too. It was so hard to see them go. I went down at 7am to see them off. Roy, George, Bud, Bill, Chuck, Fred, Ron, Basil, Bib, Mickey—over all of them, Les. Kids I grew up with almost—some hardly 18, some 17. They have all gone for active service they say in the papers. Gosh, I hated to see them go.

ଔ King, Molly, her sister Betty and the deer. (circa 1939)

Building Our House

After Molly and I got engaged in 1937, I started to think about building a house. My dad gave me the property next door to his place. He said it would make a good building site after I cleared it.

After I blew the stumps, I got Mr. Knobs in with his logging horses. They pulled out the roots and put them into piles so that I could burn them.

My next challenge was to get lumber for the house. Bill McAfee had a sawmill on top of Mount Bruce. I asked him if I could work in the mill in exchange for lumber. He agreed to hire me—if I had a truck. I traded in my car for a three and a half tonne REO speed wagon.

Molly and I with our REO speed wagon. (1937)

I started working at the sawmill in April. Around the first of August, Mr. McAfee wanted to move the sawmill from Mount Bruce to Fulford. I helped him take the mill apart and I hauled it down the hill in my REO speed wagon. We rebuilt the sawmill on the waterfront to the south of where Drummond Children's Playground now stands.

I remember the first morning I started work at the new site. Mr. McAfee had hired a young fellow by the name of Wilf Kitchen, who had just moved to Salt Spring from Saskatchewan. Mr. McAfee was the sawyer and he needed a man to help him roll the logs onto the carriage.

Mr. Kitchen had never done this type of work before and I heard him ask what he should do. Mr. McAfee said, "Just watch me and do whatever I do." He gave Mr. Kitchen a cant hook and each man stood at opposite ends of the log and began to roll it.

On the first try, Mr. Kitchen's cant hook shifted and Mr. McAfee took all the weight. After about three unsuccessful tries, Mr. McAfee got so angry that he threw his cant hook up against the wall. Mr. Kitchen immediately threw his cant hook too, but it went out the window and landed on the beach.

“What did you do that for?” Mr. McAfee demanded.

Mr. Kitchen replied, “Well, you told me to do whatever you did!”

Working at the sawmill from April to the end of December, I got enough lumber to build my house from the basement up to the first floor. Unfortunately, Mr. McAfee wouldn’t let me have any of the good lumber. I had to take my wood from the cull lumber that was not good enough for export.

When I was ready to frame my house, I talked to Gilbert Mouat, of Mouat Bros., about buying some lumber. Gilbert had a lumber yard. He said that they had a pile of rough lumber that was left behind when a mill was moved out of the Cranberry. I bought the whole pile for a reasonable price and got enough lumber to frame my house.

Trading work with our friends and family helped us a lot. Molly’s father and our neighbour, Jack Graham, who were both carpenters, helped us build the house, put in windows and build fireplaces and chimneys. I returned the favour by plowing their fields with my horses and putting in their crops.

When the Kelloggs came back that summer, Molly and I left the farm and moved into my parents’ place up the road for a couple of weeks until we got our house ready.

When we moved in, our house still needed quite a bit of work. The basement hadn’t been boarded in yet and we hadn’t put a door on the stairs leading down to the basement. There was a lot of ventilation! To stop the draught coming up the stairs, we hung an old blanket over the doorway. That blanket sure did swing when the wind blew! We were happy to move in none-the-less and worked on the house full time for a few months to get it fixed up.

ঔ Our house on Fulford-Ganges Road, the day we moved in, and my best dog, King. (1939)

Actually, we worked on the house for years, changing it here, changing it there, adding on here and there. After each baby came, we added another room. Molly liked kids and she was always glad to have another baby. The kids were coming along pretty fast, so we put up a lot of additions!

In the 1940s I built three bedrooms upstairs and, over the years, I made quite a few additions to the original house. I added on to the kitchen to make a larger dining area and another bedroom downstairs. Off the living room, I added a guest bedroom that I also used to store all my firearms. Later, Molly used that room when she began her doll collection. In the early 1950s I added a large family room with a huge stone fireplace. That room was a good place for the children to play and it was great for family gatherings and parties. All in all, we didn't do too badly—everybody had their own bed, at least.

Over the years, Molly and I had eleven children:

- Darlene (born April 30, 1940),
- Robert Edward (Ted) (born December 2, 1941),
- Roberta (born January 6, 1943),
- Merilyn (Lyn) (born July 22, 1944),
- Morris (Morry) (born May 31, 1947),
- Catherine (Cathy) (born April 21, 1949),
- Daniel (Dan) (born March 28, 1951),
- Patrick (Pat) (born April 15, 1954),
- James (Jim) (born June 9, 1955),
- Kerry (born July 16, 1957), and
- Lance (born November 9, 1958).

Making Adjustments

I learned early on in our marriage that my life was going to be different than it was when I was living with Mom and Dad. Molly made it clear that I had some adjustments to make.

When Molly and I moved into our new house, there was a ball diamond across the street. I came home one day to see the boys out there playing ball. They asked me to join them and, even though I knew that I should have gone in and straightened up the house with Molly, I just couldn't let the boys down. Boy! Did I ever get bawled out when I got home!

After that, I noticed that Molly didn't have much to say to me for a while. I got that more than once—I often had to ask Molly what was going on. She explained that I was getting the silent treatment. When I thought about it, I always figured out why and I knew that I deserved it.

After learning a few things the hard way, I made some adjustments and, since I was always busy with logging, working the sheep and whatever else I got into, I guess I didn't get on Molly's nerves very much by hanging around the house. I think that suited her fine most of the time.

When I was pulling off something she didn't like, Molly straightened me out fast. She wouldn't hesitate to bawl me out if I was out of line! Otherwise, we got along quite well and she kept me and all of our children in order.

Raising Our Family

As young parents, Molly and I had a lot of excitement and good times with our family. I could never remember all of the funny things that each of them have said and done, but a few stories do stick in my mind and still bring a smile.

Our first child, Darlene, gave us an early taste of what life with children would be like. When she was a baby, she was always reaching for things and saying, "I want!" In fact, those were some of her first words. One night I showed her the full moon in the sky. It looked quite beautiful and she immediately decided that she wanted it.

I couldn't pacify her with toys or anything, until I had a great idea. I got a grapefruit from the cupboard and pretended that I had pulled it from the sky. I gave it to Darlene and she was finally happy. Nothing but the moon from the sky could satisfy her that night!

Later, when Darlene was about three years old, she swallowed a bobby pin. Molly and I were quite scared when she started to choke, but Darlene eventually got it down and swallowed it. We watched for it for a few days and, when we saw that it had gone through her, we were relieved to know that she was safe. To make sure it wouldn't happen again, Molly tried to talk with Darlene about the incident. “Why,” she asked, “did you swallow that bobby pin?”

“Teddy told me to!” Darlene insisted. With the look of innocence on her face, we might have believed her, except that Teddy was only one year old at the time and couldn't talk yet.

Darlene, Roberta and Ted in front of our farm. (circa 1944)

Discipline

With so many kids in the house, we had to set some ground rules to make sure that nothing got out of control. We had some basic, common sense rules that just could not be broken. For example, each child knew that they could never pick on anyone younger. This simple rule cut out a lot of fights and arguments. Most of the time, our kids were really good and they looked after one another. Sometimes though, the rules had to be enforced. Maybe it was because I was away from home so much, but Molly was definitely more strict with the kids than I was.

One time I was working at the back of the house when little Merilyn came running, yelling “Daddy! Daddy! Daddy!”

She was only four years old and I thought, “Gosh, something terrible has happened!” I asked her what was wrong, but she was so upset she didn’t answer. I grabbed her in my arms and held her tight.

Next thing I knew, Molly came running around the corner of the house—and she was after Lynie! Lynie must have said something cheeky to Molly and when Molly took after her, Lynie just ran.

Even though I had picked up Lynie, Molly kept a’coming after us. I didn’t know what to do! I spotted a big stinging nettle patch nearby. Molly was wearing shorts and since I had my jeans on, I thought the best thing I could do was to get in the middle of that patch and save Lynie!

I ran into the middle of the nettles holding Lynie up high so she wouldn’t get stung. There was Molly on the outside of the patch, just bawling Lynie out to beat heck. Eventually Molly got tired of talking and went back into the house and I got Lynie out of the nettles.

This sign still hangs in my kitchen.

Fair Play

We always aimed to make life at home as fair for our kids as we could. Sometimes, when I saw that one child was at a disadvantage, I'd step in and try to help the situation.

I remember when Jim was about three, the kids were all playing cops and robbers around the house. Jim was putting a lot of energy into running after everyone who came by, but he was getting frustrated because all the older kids were shooting him before he had a chance to shoot.

I could see he was getting down about it, so I took him aside and gave him some advice. On my suggestion, he hid in the corner of the house where the other kids couldn't see him.

It took some patience, but little Jim stood there, grinning with anticipation, for his chance to get one of the big kids. When the first one ran by, Jim jumped out and yelled "bang!" I don't know who was more surprised: Jim for finally getting one of the big kids, or Ted, who wasn't used to being tricked by his little brother!

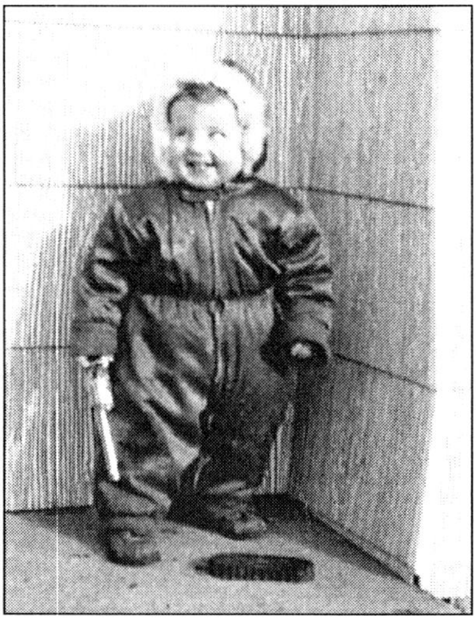

ଔ Jim Akerman, age three, playing cops and robbers. (circa 1958)

ଔ Molly and the kids getting ready to head into town. Back: Ted, Roberta, Molly, Lyn and Darlene. Front: Morris, Dan and Cathy. (circa 1952)

Saving Money

With at least eleven kids in the house at any one time, Molly and I did our best to stretch our dollars as far as they would go. Like most families in the area, and just like I had been raised to do by my parents, we lived off the land. We also found some other inventive ways to save money—some were more popular than others!

Molly spent a lot of time making sure we were all well fed. In the summer she preserved food for us to eat through the winter. Each year she canned about one hundred bottles of cherries, not to mention all the other fruit and vegetables she did up. She used the big Mason quart and a half jars.

Molly canned venison too. She cut it into squares, browned it in the frying pan and put it in jars. She cooked the jars in a big pressure cooker. The venison lasted all winter.

The kids often asked what we were going to have for supper. Molly would often say "Venison stew!" and sing, "Venison stew, venison stew, venison stew for a change!" We had it a lot!

While Molly was saving us money on food, I tried to save us money on haircuts. I set up my own barbershop, with a chair and all the tools, where I gave all the kids haircuts. I didn't have any formal training, but most of my haircuts turned out pretty good. I'm afraid that Roberta might say otherwise after one of the cuts I gave her!

When she started school, Roberta had long hair that Molly used to have to fiddle with every morning. When Molly started to get fed up with it, I decided to make everyone's lives easier.

ᏩᏕ My mom, dad and relatives, posing for a picture on the stairs of our house. Back: Molly Carlin, Sheila Carlin, Howard Carlin, Roberta Akerman, Molly Akerman, me, Bill Harris, Dorothy Harris, Ellen Akerman and Jim Akerman. Middle: Terry Akerman, George Edward (Ted) Akerman, Pauline Harris, Diane Carlin, Darlene Akerman and Brian Brenton. Front: Clare Harris, Ted Akerman, David Harris and Wesley Akerman. (circa 1946)

I sat Roberta down in the barber chair and set to work. First, I cut a thick set of bangs straight across her forehead, extending them back over her ears. This was a good start, but the back was still long and I knew it would be a lot of trouble to keep neat. The cleanest, easiest style I could think of was the one I gave to the boys, so I cut the back short, just like her brothers' cuts.

Without a mirror to look in, Roberta sat patiently until I was done. I thought it looked nice and neat, and was pleased to show Roberta her new look. Upon her first glance in the mirror, Roberta shrieked.

I was still optimistic that Molly would like it, considering how easy it would be to take care of, but the look on her face made it clear that, starting right away, Roberta would be growing her hair long again.

Patterson's Store

Like many people on Salt Spring, Molly and I didn't get regular paycheques. Although we worked hard all year round, we didn't get paid until the whole job was done. I farmed sheep all year, but it was only when I was able to take the lambs to Vancouver in June that I got any money for the work. Same thing with logging: I didn't get paid until the 'boom was sold' or until the truckloads of Christmas trees were shipped. As a result, Molly and I relied on our savings for most of the year and sometimes we found ourselves a little short.

Our family was always thankful for the generosity of Mr. and Mrs. Patterson, who owned Patterson's Store in Fulford. Will Patterson ran the store with his wife Emma and their son Bob. Bob and his wife Nancy eventually took over the store, but Old Mr. Patterson was very involved in the store for many more years.

When Molly and I were raising our family, the Pattersons took orders over the phone and delivered groceries and other goods right to our door. For many years, the Pattersons delivered to customers throughout the south end of the island including Fulford Valley, Beaver Point and Isabella Point. The delivery service was much appreciated, but it was the Patterson's generosity that earned the family a special place in our hearts.

Often, the Pattersons allowed their customers to run a bill until they were able to pay. They never asked for payment or refused more goods. Patterson's was a well-stocked little general store that sold everything that people needed to survive including groceries, animal feed, coal oil and candles, fishing and hunting equipment and more. They carried some people for many months and never charged interest. The Pattersons saved many Fulford residents, including our family, from hard times.

Patterson's Store is still run by Mr. and Mrs. Will Patterson's grandson, Bruce Patterson. Like his grandparents and parents, Bruce runs a well-stocked little store. It is a real asset to locals and travellers alike.

Stories! I Want Stories!

When I had a long day driving the logging truck, I came home from work just exhausted. I was too tired to eat, sometimes. I got home around six o'clock and stumbled to the couch to lie down. First thing, at least four kids were on top of me. They pounded away, wanting me to tell them stories! "STORIES! I want stories! I want STORIES!"

Through all that I could fall sound asleep. Molly often wondered how I could sleep with those kids climbing all over me, but on those days I could sleep through anything!

When I wasn't so tired, the kids rested on my pillow while I told them stories. Sometimes, while they lay there with their eyes closed, listening to every word, I told them about the werewolf that lived in the mountains. When they were calm and enjoying the story, I would yell, "Oh, I think I hear him coming now!" They pressed their eyes tighter together and sunk down closer to the pillow. To get them real worried, I would add "Oh-oh! He's looking in the window!" After a couple seconds I would say "Oh, he's gone now!" and they'd run to the window, but of course, by the time they got there, the werewolf had already run away. They were scared of that werewolf—even though they never saw him.

Other times I told them stories about the animals that lived on Salt Spring. When I was a boy, my parents gave me Thornton Burgess books to read. Mr. Burgess' wonderful stories described the lives of the animals in the forest and combined good fun stories with some lessons about life.

The stories I told my children incorporated places they recognized on our farm, but the characters and their names were influenced by those Burgess books that I loved as a child. I borrowed Mr. Burgess' famous names—Buster Bear, Paddy the Beaver, Peter Rabbit and Chatter the Red Squirrel, for example—and I told my stories as though my dad was Farmer Brown and I was Farmer Brown's boy. The kids really liked those stories and they learned a lot about the animals that lived on the island.

Sometimes, I had help telling stories. I had a little monkey puppet that couldn't talk very well, but he could nod yes or no. When the monkey, or 'The Mighty,' as Lynie called him when she was young, was out for a visit, the kids gathered around to see what wisdom he had to share. He always knew if one of them had been good—or bad—and that was enough to get them interested in what he had to say. That monkey always managed to stir up some trouble and get them laughing!

ଓ 'Monkey' hams for the camera.

Play Time

It didn't happen often, but sometimes I came home from work to find the kids intent on doing their own thing; the younger ones enjoyed playing games like cops and robbers and hide and seek, while the older ones had their school work and sports. Molly and I encouraged them all to play together and to get outside and get some exercise. Sometimes, when we least expected it, we found great humour in our kids' everyday experiences and comments.

For a couple of weeks every summer our children attended lessons with the nuns from St. Anne's Academy in Victoria, who came to Salt Spring Island to teach the catechism.

Molly and I often talked with the kids about their lessons over supper to see what they had learned and what they found interesting. One lesson in particular had made an impact on the children. Their attention was caught by the phrase: “Man came from dust and to dust he shall return.”

A few days later some of the children were playing hide and seek in our bedroom. Mid-game, Cathy called out, “Mommy! Mommy! Come quick!” Thinking something was terribly wrong, Molly rushed into the room. When she got there, Cathy pointed at some dust bunnies under the bed and shouted, “Look! Somebody’s either coming or going!”

Hide and seek prompted another funny moment when my cousin, Pat Brenton, found the ultimate hiding spot. A bunch of kids were playing the game in my parents’ yard while the adults were visiting. When it was time to hide, this little guy found the best spot of all—under Grandmother Akerman’s long, dark skirt. Grandmother stood still, but the folds of her skirt moved ever so slightly as the familiar call rang out: “Ready or not, you shall be caught—hiding around the base or not!” Pat hid there quite a long time, to the frustration of the poor kid trying to find him, but he finally burst out just as that kid was walking by.

When he was tagged, he stood up for himself by saying: “You never would have found me if Grandmother hadn’t let one go!”

Boxing, Round Two

When my boys were teenagers, I encouraged them to box. I even built a gymnasium in our house so they would have a place to practice. When they were training, they boxed in there every night. They had all their friends over in the evening to work out in our gymnasium.

When Ted was sixteen, he fought boys who were older and stronger than he was—and he beat them! He beat George Henry who went on to become the Canadian Champion and he beat Clear Sky, who was the Canadian Army Champion at that time.

When Ted fought George Henry, the Vancouver Island Golden Gloves Champion, George had a lot more experience. But Ted remembered his lessons and did what he had to do to win.

The same thing happened when he fought Clear Sky. Clear Sky was a tough fighter. He headbutted Ted in the very first round! Ted was bleeding so badly that they rescheduled the match.

Ted spent the next month training and figuring out how to beat Clear Sky at his own game. I taught him a trick I'd learned when I was boxing: hit the heavy bag and then miss it on purpose, but come back and hit it again with his elbow.

The second fight with Clear Sky was shaping up just like the first one. When Clear Sky tried to headbutt him, Ted used the heavy-bag trick he had practiced so many times over the past month and hit him square in the ear with his elbow. Once Clear Sky knew he couldn't get away with headbutting, Ted had no trouble winning the fight.

I was happy to teach my boys the same sorts of tricks my coaches taught me. The boys learned their lessons well. They boxed in Vancouver, Victoria, and Nanaimo amongst other places. All of our boys were Golden Gloves—BC Champions. Building that room for them paid off in the end for them and their friends.

Dan and Morris Akerman with their boxing trophies. (circa 1960) Photo credit: *Gulf Islands Driftwood*

Dancing

Sometimes, Molly and I got away from home for a little playtime of our own. We liked to go to Vancouver to visit friends and, occasionally, go dancing. This picture is from a memorable night at one of Vancouver's popular nightspots—the Cave Supper Club:

Molly and I at the Cave Supper Club in Vancouver. Molly's sister, Peggy, wrote on the border: "You can take us out of the country, but you can't take the country out of us." (circa 1950)

Christmas

When I was a kid, I couldn't wait for Santa Claus come to our house. For Christmas Dad always cut down a pine tree and set it up in the living room. Mom decorated the boughs with real candles that we lit on Christmas Eve.

My brother Jim always woke me up in the middle of the night so we could go downstairs to see what we got in our stockings. I remember plainly what we got: an orange, some raisins, some nuts and, once in a while, I got a popgun that shot corks out the end. That was always neat!

While I was in school we had special Christmas concerts every year. Through the weeks leading up to the big event, we practiced our play and sang songs. The night of the concert, our families came to the school to watch us perform. We were all dressed up and very serious about doing a good job for our parents. After we finished our performance, the adults pushed all the desks back against the walls of the school room so the really young children and the babies could sleep on the floor, behind the desks. The rest of us waited for Santa Claus to come.

The first year I saw Santa at school, somebody opened the window for him and he crawled through with a sack full of toys in his hand. Right away I noticed that he was holding a teddy bear. Boy, I thought, I'd sure like to have that! When it was time for Santa to give out his toys, he called out my name and gave me the teddy bear. I was so excited! This is for ME! I was pretty proud of that teddy bear and I took him to bed every night. I wouldn't go to sleep without him. I've had that bear since 1916 and now he has a special place in our house.

ଔ My sister-in-law, Peggy Bryan, wrote a little story about my bear:

Bob's Teddy

by Peggy Bryan (nee Morrison), March 15, 1978

At this point in my life, I am very, very happy!! As a young cub I was loved so much—I was taken everywhere, I was taken for long walks—over fences and through fields, with grass higher than 'he' was, across the bridge over to the big barn. Sixty years ago, the hill did indeed look steep and the barn was SO big it went on forever.

I remember one afternoon I got left in the barn, night came and still I was there. 'He' didn't like going to bed that night without me, but no one could find me. I was about the same colour as the straw I was lying on. The next morning, 'his' mom found me, when she came in to milk the cows.

My paws got worn and someone, lovingly, put new ones on me—in pretty plaid. Still later, someone gave me a vest of warm rabbit skin because all of my fur was just about worn off.

'He' thought 'he' didn't need me anymore, so I got put in the attic and that is where I was for many years. I'd lost some of my head stuffing, one ear was hanging by a thread, almost lost it, my nose was gone, but my eyes—though not sitting quite at the right angle—were still bright.

What a joy it was, one day to see 'him' come and pick me up and say, "poor teddy." I just wasn't feeling too perky, and didn't feel much like being shown off.

'He' thought maybe a new coat might be the answer—so—over the old, the almost new coat was put on and my own bright eyes looked me over and I thought I looked like quite a handsome fellow.

<u>Now</u> I'll have my picture taken with 'him' and I'll be looked after for a long, long time. I am a little frail and can't stand the busy days of a small human anymore, but I can enjoy being admired and the wonderful stories told about me, will keep me very, <u>VERY</u> happy!!!

☙ Me and my favourite teddy bear (circa 2003)

Christmas with the Children

Molly and I enjoyed making special times for our children to remember and Christmas was especially fun. We always had a big Christmas. While the children knew we were celebrating Jesus' birthday, the young ones also enjoyed Santa Claus.

One year, when our son Dan was about six, some of his school friends told him that there was no such thing as

Santa. Dan didn't want to give up on Santa, but he was beginning to believe his friends. It was too soon for him to miss out on the fun, so I thought, "Well, I'll fool you!"

I had a lot of extra sheep bells, so I tied them all together on a long string. Late at night, after I figured the children were asleep I went out and grabbed my line of sheep bells from the garage. I wound up and threw them up onto the top of the roof so that I could grab hold of the string on either side of the house. I ran from one side of the house to the other, pulling that string of bells back and forth again and again so that they jingled and rang! I was sure Dan would wake up and hear the bells.

The next morning I mentioned that I thought I had heard Santa Claus on the roof, but I wasn't sure. I asked Dan, very seriously, if he heard anything unusual the night before. "Yes!" he said, excitedly. "I heard bells on the roof! I didn't believe in Santa before, but I sure do now!"

By the time the younger kids reached the age when they questioned Santa, I had to think of a new way to fool them. I used to cover a flashlight with red Christmas paper. Then, after dark when the kids were in bed, I went out to the end of the lane. From there, I rang a brass bell and shone that red light towards the house where the kids could see it. They were always sure that they had seen Rudolph's red nose on Christmas Eve!

With a house full of children that believed in Santa, he sure did get a lot of treats on Christmas Eve! The children put beer and chocolates out for Santa every year. I'm not sure how they decided that Santa would like beer and chocolates, but I do remember that I was happy to drink the beer and Molly liked to eat the chocolates!

Molly always stayed up very late on Christmas Eve., changing presents around. She worried that this child had a little more than that one, so she moved the gifts around until she was sure everything was fair. She was very particular that they were all going to get the same amount of gifts. The older girls generally got dresses and clothes and things like that to wear to school. The younger kids got trucks and bulldozers. They all had to get the same amount, though. I don't remember any of them ever saying, "Oh, you got more than I did." Molly did a good job finding everyone something that they would like.

☙ The kids opening presents on Christmas morning. Back: Ted, Darlene and Morris. Middle: Lyn, Cathy and Roberta. Front: Pat, Dan and Jim. Kerry is seated in the front. (circa 1959)

On Christmas mornings the kids got up around six or seven o'clock. They went into the kitchen for something to eat, but they just couldn't wait to get into the living room to see that Christmas tree. When everything was ready, we had the smallest one wait at the door and the others lined up behind him. Ah, their faces! They were so happy on Christmas morning!

Christmas dinner was also an event to remember. Each year about fifty of the relations came in for a big dinner. Molly did most of the cooking and she made a big turkey, with vegetables and potatoes. She started getting ready for Christmas dinner in September when she pulled out my mom's old hard-covered cookbook and made dark Christmas cake and Christmas pudding. I still have lots of visitors at Christmas, except now it's a Boxing Day dinner and I do all the cooking.

Easter

At Easter I got up to my tricks again. The children believed that the Easter Bunny would visit them and that, if they made special nests for him, he would put treats in them. In the days leading up to Easter, the kids made nests out of cotton batten, paper and whatever else they could find. Anticipation ran high, but the kids were never as excited as they were when they saw the Easter bunnies dancing.

The night before the Easter Bunny came, I snuck out of the house with some paper. I went down to the other side of the creek in the woods behind our house, crumpled up the paper and lit a fire. Once the fire got going, I went back to the house and, pointing to the fire, said, "Oh look! The Easter bunnies are having a dance down in the woods!"

The kids gathered around the window and, sure enough, they were all impressed to see the bunnies dancing around the fire. They were all convinced that they could see the bunnies dancing! Before bed, they put carrots and treats out for the Easter Bunny to thank him for the presents he was about to put in their nests.

The next morning, the children ran to their nest to see what the Easter Bunny left behind. They were thrilled to get their Easter goodies, but surprised to see bunny poos lying all over the house!

I always pretended that I was angry at the bunnies for leaving such a mess behind. Usually, one of the kids got smart and said, "That's not a bunny poo! That's a raisin!"

"If it's a raisin," I'd say, "then why don't you eat it?" Nobody ever ate a raisin on Easter morning!

Our children: Morry, Cathy, Lyn holding Jim, Darlene holding Kerry, Roberta holding Patrick, Dan and Ted. (circa 1957)

ᴄᴕ Our children on Christmas morning: Jim, Pat, Dan, Cathy, Morry, Lyn, Roberta, Ted and Darlene holding Kerry. (circa 1957)

In Bed with Chickens

Molly and I sure had fun with the kids, but we liked to have our friends and family over for some fun times too.

Every once in a while we got some friends out for a few beers and a card game. We liked to play poker and a game we called 'Ganges in the Mud.'

My cousin Ernie Brenton and his wife Ruth sometimes came over from Vancouver to visit his mother, who was my mother's sister, Mary Katherine. On those occasions, we usually expected to see them for a game of cards. On this particular night, they were pretty tired after their trip, so they wanted to have a nap before coming down to play.

They never did make it to the game, so about midnight, my son-in-law, Tim O'Donnell, who was always ready for a practical joke, said "If they won't come to our party, let's go and wake them up!"

On the way to the old Brenton house where they were staying, Tim and I passed the chicken coop of my neighbour, and tenant, Ray Simard. It seemed like a good idea to get some chickens to throw into Ruth and Ernie's bedroom! I grabbed a big red rooster and Tim grabbed a hen.

It was just after midnight, so we tried to be quiet, but as we walked away with the chickens in our hands, out came Ray Simard. "Oh! Stealing chickens, eh?" he said.

All I could say was "Yep." Ray recognized me, but he didn't say anything. He just walked back into the house.

With chickens in hand, we walked across the road to where Ernie and Ruth were staying. We had intended to throw the chickens through the window into their bedroom, but when we got around to the side of the house we saw that the window was closed.

Not ones to give up easily, we decided to take the chickens right into the house. My grannie had lived in this house for years, so I knew it very well. By the time we walked in the kitchen door, we had it figured out—we'll go in, grab the top blanket, pull it back and throw the chickens in their bed.

We tiptoed into the bedroom, holding the chickens in our arms. There was a lot of moonlight and it shone inside so we could see a little bit. Ruth and Ernie were being quite noisy, snoring, so we knew they were sound asleep.

Tim walked around to Ernie's side of the bed and I stayed on Ruth's side. According to plan, we pulled the top blanket down and I put that big old rooster right on Ruth's stomach. It hopped onto her head and she started screaming, "There's something in my hair! There's something in my hair!"

Ernie thought she was having a nightmare and tried to calm her down by saying that everything was fine and that she should go back to sleep. "There's nothing in your hair," he assured her.

"Yes there is!" Ruth screamed.

Well! You've probably never heard anybody make so much noise! Ruth was screaming and Ernie was cussing. Oh God! The words he was saying! We took that opportunity to run back outside.

Aunty Mary heard the commotion and by the time she came running out of her room Ernie was walking through the kitchen with a chicken under each arm. As he threw them out the door, Aunty Mary asked where he got the chickens. Ernie answered truthfully: "I found them in my bed, Mom."

Tim and I were hiding around the corner of the house, barely stifling our laughter, while Ernie was walking through the kitchen with the chickens. When he opened the door and tossed the chickens out onto the porch, we grabbed them.

Even on the main road, we could still hear Ruth screaming and Ernie cussing away! On the way home, we put the chickens in Ray Simard's mailbox. We were still laughing when we got back to the house.

I'm not sure who found the chickens; if she had some mail to put out the next day, Elsie Simard might have got the surprise. If not, then Frank Pyatt would have got it when he delivered the mail.

Some years later, when Ruth was visiting Aunty Mary Brenton at the extended care home in Ganges, a new patient came into the room. She took one look at Ruth and exclaimed, "If YOU'RE on the outside, what am I doing in here?"

I'm not sure if it was because of that remark or not, but later that day, Ruth went to the beauty parlour. When she got home, my daughter's father-in-law was visiting. He was deaf, so she spoke loudly when she explained that she had just been to the beauty parlour to have her hair done. He didn't answer when she asked him if he liked it, so she talked a little louder and said "Doesn't it look nice? I just paid $50 for it."

"Yep," he said, "You can't get much for $50 these days!"

Losing Lyn

Our third daughter, Merilyn, was an energetic and friendly person who put her all into everything she did. From her youth when she was very active in sports, to her adulthood while she was raising her family, Lyn was a pleasure to be around. Even though she was a busy person with lots of things on the go, she had a kind nature and always made time to help others.

As a young woman, after completing her studies in Victoria, Lyn pursued her dream of nursing and left Salt Spring Island for Port Arthur, Ontario, where she took her first job in a seniors home.

When she met her future husband, Dennis Andrews, in Port Arthur, we thought she might stay out there for good, but the lure of Salt Spring was too strong. After coming home for their honeymoon, Lyn and Dennis lasted only three more months in Port Arthur before deciding to move back to Salt Spring Island. The whole family was thrilled to have Lyn back home again.

Lyn settled back into life on the island. She enjoyed her home in Hundred Hills and made everyone feel welcome there. She was an excellent cook and gardener and she was the kind of housekeeper whose house was always clean and in order—no matter when she was surprised with a visit! Lyn loved her home and, especially, the view from the deck towards the Gulf Islands. We've always referred to that view as 'Lyn's View.'

Lyn and Dennis had three children: Rick, Jack and Michelle. Her children were the biggest joy in Lyn's life. As her children were growing up, Lyn saved their toys in anticipation of her grandchildren.

It was devastating to us all when Lyn came down with multiple sclerosis at thirty-five. Lyn stayed at home and was cared for by her family for many years before it became necessary for her to be admitted to Lady Minto Hospital here on Salt Spring.

Lyn and her family battled against the illness for eighteen years. Despite her own troubles, Lyn never complained about her lot in life. She was always ready with a smile and did her best to make her visitors feel comforted and loved. From her hospital bed, Lyn kept in touch with her friends and family and delighted in learning about their day-to-day lives and accomplishments. Lyn was especially thrilled when her grandchildren were born.

Lyn passed away at fifty-three with her family by her side. Lyn was a wonderful wife, mother, grandmother, daughter, sister and friend. Her illness never suppressed her enthusiasm for life or her love for her friends and family. She was loved by all who knew her.

☙ This is a favourite photo of our daughter Lyn. It was taken when she graduated from nursing school. (circa 1963)

Losing Molly

Besides kids and softball, suntanning was Molly's other hobby. She had a tent trailer on some property we had or the beach. In the summertime she went there and lay out in the sun, pretty near all day. She got tanned as dark as anything. I guess she got too much of a good thing.

Molly was just over eighty when she had a patch on her back that wouldn't heal. The doctor said it was shingles and gave her some salve. She used it for a couple months, but it didn't do any good. I told her to get the doctor to take a sample and send it to the lab. When he did, we found out she had skin cancer. By then it covered most of her back.

She went to the cancer clinic in Vancouver and they pretty well cured the cancer on her back, but there was one spot on her ankle that never seemed to get better. It kept going from bad to worse for about three years.

She passed away when she was eighty-four. We were just a few months shy of our 60th wedding anniversary. It would have been our diamond anniversary.

My wife, Molly Akerman. (circa 1979)

14

Sheep Farming

THE AKERMAN FAMILY HAS A LONG HISTORY OF FARMING SHEEP on Salt Spring Island. My dad got his flock from his father and turned it over to me. I, in turn, passed the sheep business to my children who are now farming sheep in some of the same pastures where my grandfather's sheep ran. All of us have had our share of experiences with a sheep farmer's worst enemies: marauding dogs and cougars. The cougar stories seem to be the most memorable.

Sheep

My dad had one hundred sheep running in the back of our house, in the hills and all the way over to Cusheon Lake. I used to drive them for him, but when I got married in 1939 he gave the sheep to me. I increased the flock gradually after that.

If an old-timer wanted to get rid of his sheep, I bought his flock and his range. Pretty soon I had sheep running from Isabella Point, right around to Burgoyne and back up to end of Rainbow Road. The runs weren't all attached, so I put in roads to move the sheep between ranges.

People always used to ask me how many sheep I had. I always told them that I didn't know because every time I tried to count them, I fell asleep!

We left the sheep out in the range all year. If there was too much snow up on the mountain, they moved down towards the water. I never lost any in the snow. Every summer we rounded up the sheep to shear them and take the lambs. If I was logging at the time, I'd take some time off work, but when I finished logging in 1958 I went right into raising sheep with the boys full time.

ଓଓ My sons Dan and Pat helped me shear the sheep. (1958)

My Two-Legged Dogs

I kept track of all the sheep with my sheep dogs and my boys. I called them my two-legged dogs! When they weren't helping Molly out at home, my girls Cathy, Darlene, Roberta and Lyn used to drive sheep too. When the kids were young, all their school friends wanted to drive sheep.

☙ My sons Jim and Pat took an early interest in the sheep. This is them in front of my farm truck. (circa 1957)

Cabin at Cape Kepple

In the summertime we went up to our cabin at Cape Kepple for the weekends to drive and shear sheep. Sometimes we had ten kids camping with us. I bought ten loaves of bread at a time. And pork and beans by the gallon tin! Lots of times we got some young grouse on our way to the cabin. The kids got a big kick out of roasting them on the fire.

The sheep used to roam off several hundred acres in small bunches. We spread out around them and walked in, bringing them all ahead of us until the small bunches gathered into one big herd. I had set up a fenced area with a lead fence running up the mountain to encourage the sheep to walk into the corral. When they hit the fence they couldn't get away so they came right down into my corrals, where we sheared the sheep and took the lambs. Generally, we drove two hundred sheep off the east range at once, but one time we brought in more than two hundred and forty of them. That line of sheep sure did stretch out a long way!

In the summertime we got up at daylight to do a couple of drives while it was still cool outside. We tried to work from daylight till about eleven o'clock, when it got too hot. Everybody was ready for a rest by then anyways, so they got under a maple tree and had a nap. It was pretty tough work and, since they usually stayed up late around the campfire, they slept most of the afternoon. While they slept, I cooked their lunch. We ate pork and beans, canned meat, boiled potatoes and a lot of canned stew. I fed them pretty good. When it cooled down around four o'clock in the afternoon, I shouted at them, "OK boys, we'll have a cup of tea and head out!" We went at it again until dark.

There were lots of stories around the campfire when we were herding sheep. My nephew, Peter Harris, was quite a joker. He's a schoolteacher in Victoria now, but when he was out with us on the range, he was a great fella for ghost stories. He could tell them one after the other until he had those kids scared to go to bed!

Pat was about eight when he started. He was the youngest one to help. The oldest kid was probably fourteen years old. I was always telling them, "We can't start driving too early this morning because there's too much dew on the grass. If Pat gets out in that tall grass, he'll drown!" He was the smallest one out there, but Pat got to be the fastest on the mountain.

I always had to be sure I had some bandages in the truck for all those kids. I always bought special leather boots with soft rubber soles for our kids because I didn't want them to hurt their feet on the sharp rocks. We called them 'chase boots'. The other kids didn't always have good footwear for sheeping, so I had lots of bandages for the blisters they got on their feet. Even with sore feet, those kids would be out there, running all over the mountain!

I paid them all 25 cents an hour for as long as they were out there. The wages weren't very high, but they thought it was good because, otherwise they wouldn't have made anything. I used to work for 25 cents an hour myself, so I didn't feel so bad about paying them that much. Some of them made maybe $5 in a weekend. They were very pleased they were able to get something.

The day after our drive, I loaded our double-deck truck with about eighty-five lambs and got the first ferry to the mainland. I drove over to Swifts in New Westminster, or sometimes into Canada Packers in Vancouver, where I weighed the lambs and took their weight up to the office. They paid around $15-16 a head, right there.

Near the end, I had about a thousand sheep. If it wasn't for the children, I wouldn't have been able to handle that many sheep on the range. With the children helping, we were able to make a living.

When I retired from driving sheep, I divided up my land and gave it to our kids. That's how they got their start.

Driving Sheep

A lot of the school kids that helped us have left the island to work and raise their families, but when they come back, they generally come in to see me. The first thing they want to talk about is the days when we were driving sheep. It just sticks in their mind, the things we used to do!

One day I had a visit from a retired teacher who had worked for me years ago for 25 cents an hour. When I introduced this chap to a friend, he mentioned that he had helped me drive sheep in the early days. “Yeah, that Bob!” he said. “He only paid me 5 cents an hour!”

That wasn’t right, but I let it go because he walked right into it. I said, “Well you know, I always paid them what they were worth! If they weren’t working very much, I didn’t pay them very much.”

Sheep Drive

Sesame Street

Thanks to Sesame Street, the whole world has had the opportunity to see our family’s farming operation. In the late 1970s a film crew came to Salt Spring to shoot a short piece on sheep farming.

Danny’s youngest daughter, Charlotte, and Pat’s eldest daughter, Cathy, pretended they were city girls arriving at Fulford Harbour to visit their grandfather on a sheep farm. I met them at the dock and drove them to Pat’s place where they fed the sheep.

Sesame Street eventually bought the film and now people from Montreal to Australia have seen the Akerman family sheep farming operation on Salt Spring Island.

In my favourite part of the piece, my granddaughters were talking between themselves. One girl asked the other a tough question. She gave it some serious thought for a second or two, but had no luck figuring out the answer. Eventually, she replied, "I don't know. You should ask Granddad. He knows everything." I always thought that sounded pretty good on television!

Cougars

Although we don't have very many of them around anymore, cougars were quite a threat for the early settlers. Cougars that swam over to our island have killed a lot of livestock, and sometimes children, before they were tracked down and shot.

Grannie Gyves told me my first cougar story. Her mother's friend, a lady from the Saanich band, put her baby down to sleep under a tree while she picked blackberries above Fulford. When she went back to check on the baby, it was gone. She found cougar tracks on a trail, but she never found the baby.

As you know, my Grandmother Akerman had her own troubles with cougars. Some time after a cougar showed too much interest in baby Fanny, Grandmother and Granddad Akerman came too close for comfort to another hungry cat.

They were bringing home some chickens that they had bought from their neighbours, Mr. and Mrs. Furness, who lived about a mile away. About half way home, Grandmother looked back along the trail and saw a big cougar following them. She shouted to Granddad that if the cougar got any closer, she was going to drop the chickens. She thought this would distract the cougar long enough for them to escape. Granddad obviously didn't think it was worth the price because his reply was short: "Don't drop the chickens!" Eventually, Granddad put down his chickens and beat a tree with a stick until the cougar went away.

Fulford Harbour

Mr. Soule, who lived on the hill above the White House Hotel at Fulford Harbour, once saw a cougar walking along the road in front of the hotel. He watched it cross the bridge and disappear up the mountain. Mr. Soule came and asked Dad for some help.

Dad was happy to help, but he knew his small dog wouldn't likely track the cougar, so he got Uncle Mike to come with his gordon setter.

There was snow on the ground so they had no trouble finding the cougar tracks. The dogs ran ahead. About half a mile up the mountain they came across snow that was all churned up with cougar and dog tracks. The cougar had run about a hundred yards and climbed a tree.

My dad, who was a very good shot, hit the cougar right between the eyes. When he mounted the head and skin, the hole from the thirty-thirty bullet was as clear as day.

Dad kept the cougar pelt and gave Uncle Mike the $40 bounty on the cougar.

Mount Bruce

When I was quite young, a cougar got into Uncle Mike's pigpen, killed a half grown pig and jumped the fence with it. A few weeks later Mr. Branford, who had a farm on Mount Bruce, heard his mare neighing and went to investigate. He found his half grown horse dead in the pasture with teeth marks on its throat. The tracks of a large cougar were clear in the snow around the dead horse.

Mr. Branford came down off the mountain right away and told my dad. Dad got his friend Dave Maxwell and they went up the mountain to hunt down the cougar.

They found the tracks and followed them for about a mile until they went under a large fallen cedar tree. Dad and Mr. Maxwell got up on the end of the tree and started walking toward the centre with Mr. Maxwell in the lead. Cougars are known to spring twenty to thirty feet in one jump, so they were prepared in case the cougar tried to pounce on them.

Dad saw it happen: a yellow-brown streak suddenly jumped out from under the windfall! Dave, who was a crack shot, hit the cougar before it hit the ground.

There weren't a lot of cougars around when I was growing up, but they were attracted over here again in the 1940s. People had been raising goats on the side of the mountain. Eventually the goats went wild and spread all along the mountain overlooking Vancouver Island. The cougars on Vancouver Island could probably smell them and hear them bleating. Whatever it was, the cougars were attracted enough to swim all the way over to Salt Spring. Once they got here, they feasted on the goats and, eventually, became interested in the sheep and other livestock.

Maxwell Park

I was in my thirties when I got my first cougar. Mr. Ted Carter, who had a farm close to Maxwell Park, was looking out his window when he saw a large cougar in his chicken run. He went next door to John Rogers' place and phoned me. I, in turn, phoned my friend Wally Butler from Sooke who had a good cougar hound. When I reached him at ten o'clock that night, he told me to send a boat to meet him at Swartz Bay in an hour.

We drove up to Mr. Carter's place and found the chicken run full of feathers and half a dozen dead chickens. Wally's hound, Pluto, was a black and tan with some bloodhound in him. He had a very good nose, but he wasn't as fast as some hounds are.

Pluto had been tracking the cougar around the top of Mount Maxwell for about two hours when we hit an area where a lot of trees had been blown down. Wally suggested we wait for daylight before going in, since cougars will wait in a windfall and jump on the hound as it passes under the tree.

We passed the time by talking about the old basketball days. Wally's Saanich team was closely matched with my Fulford team, so we had played some good matches in our day! After our games, we always had a dance and served bootleg wine to our guests. Wally and I had lots of stories from the old days to share while we waited for the sun to rise.

At daylight we resumed our hunt for the cougar. We circled the windfall area and spotted the cougar coming out the other side. Within minutes Pluto had him up a large fir tree. We tied Pluto out of the way, which is common practice amongst cougar hunters because a wounded cougar sometimes attacks the dog with no warning. Then we shot the cougar out of the tree and watched it fall into some small trees.

We untied Pluto and expected to walk down and pick up the cougar, but when we got there, it was gone. There was a lake below us, so Wally walked down to see if the cougar took to the water.

While I hunted around where the cougar fell, the dog caught the cougar's track and followed it into a large patch of salal. The cougar was waiting and it pounced on Pluto.

Hearing the growling and barking, I scrambled up to save Pluto, who seemed to be losing his fight. I couldn't shoot at the cougar for fear I would hit the dog, so I grabbed Pluto by the tail and tried to pull him away from the cougar. When the cougar saw me, he let go of the dog and turned to have a go at me! That was the end of the cougar, though. I shot it point blank.

☙ Pluto, Wally Butler and me with the cougar from Maxwell Park. (circa 1940s)

Since Wally came over, we have caught about two dozen cougars on Salt Spring Island. Cougars pose a threat to the livestock on the island and, because they are so unpredictable, they are a threat to people—adults and children—too. We always wanted to get rid of them before they caused any more trouble. I could probably write a whole book about cougar hunting!

Three in One Week

Our family had a particularly busy time one summer when three cougars were killed in one week: my son Ted and Father Mudge hunted the first one above Fulford on the Bryant property; some of my sons and Gavin Reynolds got the second one at Arnell Park on Stewart Road; and my sons Pat, Danny and my cousin Ernie Brenton's son, Bruce, shot the third one under Mount Maxwell.

The last cougar got some attention because the boys were so young when they bagged it. We were still tracking the cougar when it jumped off a ledge onto a tree. We followed the track to the ledge, where we saw the cougar in the tree, directly across from us. Pat, Dan and Bruce raised their rifles, took aim and, at the count of three, shot the cougar out of the tree. This story made it into newspapers all across Canada.

ଔ My sons, Pat and Dan, with Bruce Brenton. (circa 1964)
Photo credit: Agnes Flett, *The Victoria Daily Times*

A local cartoonist for Vancouver Island's paper, *The Victoria Daily Times*, drew a cartoon about it:

ଔ This cartoon, by Bob Bierman of *The Victoria Daily Times*, was based on Pat, Dan and Bruce's cougar hunting trip. In the caption, 'Molly' says: "How many times do I have to tell you kids—first your homework, and THEN you can have fun!...?" Courtesy Bob Bierman

15

Gypo Logging

I WAS NEVER MUCH GOOD AT WORKING FOR OTHER PEOPLE. I always preferred to set my own hours and make my own deals—for good and for bad. I learned some lessons the hard way, but all in all, the lifestyle suited me and it supported me and my family just fine. As with most jobs, logging allowed me to meet lots of people and form solid friendships; however, logging may have brought with it more risks and adventures than most other jobs. Fortunately, I was lucky and have nothing but fond memories of the people and the times we had together out in the bush.

Maurice McTighe

Between 1948 and 1950, I was in business with my brother-in-law Maurice McTighe. We bought a sawmill and sawed railroad ties, which we sold to outfits all over the world. We hired a truck to transport our ties down to Fulford Harbour where they were put onto ships destined for Victoria. In Victoria, the ties were moved to other ships that were headed to Vancouver and even as far away as Australia. The costs involved with trucking the ties to the harbour and then loading and shipping them to market were very high and we hardly made enough profit to justify the effort. It was a lot of work and it didn't provide a very good return. After a couple of years, Maurice and I both decided to move on to other things.

ᴄᴙ Maurice McTighe and Ken Tahouney cutting lumber at our sawmill. (circa 1949)

Tahouney Logging Company

In 1950 I joined Ken Tahouney in the Tahouney Logging Company, which he had started with his father, and formed a partnership to log timber that I had on some property above Ganges. Ken had a donkey machine to do the yarding and we hired a truck to do the hauling.

A Truck of Our Own

After my bad experience shipping cut timber, we decided to buy a truck of our own and put the logs straight into the water. We didn't have a lot of money to spend, but we went to Vancouver and bought a 1942 GMC 6x6 that needed a lot of work. Then we bought an eleven tonne Columbia tandem trailer that had very bad vacuum brakes. It wasn't the best equipment available, but it was all we could afford. All we needed now was a logging truck driver.

We got in touch with a hiring hall in Victoria and they sent us up an 'experienced trucker.' The next day we were ready to load at a cold deck. We put a small load on the truck and our 'experienced' driver started for the beach. When he reached his first steep hill, he let 'er fly! He didn't gear down enough and when he couldn't make the corner at the bottom of the hill, the truck landed in the ditch with a broken reach. The trailer hadn't tipped, but it was twisted around to face the wrong direction.

Ken and I got to work to fix up the mess. After making a new reach out of a small log, we straightened the trailer wheels and set the wooden reach in place. Somehow, without even taking the load off the truck, we fixed the trailer so it was ready to continue to the beach.

By this time, our truck driver was long gone. Ken wondered who was going to take the load to the dump. I offered to give it a try and, although I hadn't ever driven a logging truck before, I put it in low gear and made it to the harbour. That's when my hair started to turn grey!

Businessmen

For the next ten years that Ken and I worked together, I drove the logging truck and he was high rigger and donkey puncher. Between us, we did our own mechanic work too. Ken was good with the donkey and could mend the cables better than most loggers could. I was a bit of a mechanic, so I looked after our truck.

For the twelve years that I ran the logging truck, the brakes were never very good. I always made sure the brakes on my trailer were in good shape, though. I got through it somehow, anyways. I'm like a cat, I guess. I have nine lives.

Ken and I thought it was worth all the trouble because we made a lot more money than we would have made working for wages.

Before we got together, Ken had a private company backing his logging operation. When he didn't have the money to pay a crew, he borrowed money from the company against the value of his timber. They sold the logs, kept their share and gave him the money that was left.

When I had the mill, I worked through the Bank of Commerce. If I needed money to buy machinery or anything, they lent me the money and I paid them back as soon as I sold the lumber.

When I went with Ken, he switched over to the bank; they lent us whatever we wanted. We got along a lot better that way because we didn't have to pay such a large percentage of what we made. The bank just lent us the money and we paid them back. They made a little, of course, but they didn't make as much as the private company Ken had been using.

I was pretty fortunate to have a good relationship with the bank. If I found some land that somebody wanted to sell, I'd go to the bank and borrow money for a down payment. That way, I was able to come into quite a bit of land.

In those days, you could buy a piece of property and sell it for a good profit because the taxes weren't nearly what they are today. I had land on the side of the mountain and, at one time, I even had a mile and a half of waterfront, until I sold it again.

Quite early, when I first started speculating land, I bought half a mile of waterfront at Isabella Point for $1,600. A chap who wanted it came along, so I thought, "Oh, if I get $3,000 then I'll be all right," so I sold it for $3,000. Today the same land is worth a couple million. More often, though, we logged the timber off the land that I bought.

Me with a load of logs in front of our house on Fulford-Ganges Road. (circa 1952)

Loggers

Ken and I did a lot of the work ourselves, but sometimes we needed some help. If we were yarding and loading at the same time, we hired more men. That was always an adventure because, although loggers in those days were hard workers, they also liked to drink and get into a few friendly fights. Most of all, they had a great sense of humour that made working with them a lot of fun.

One day Ken and I were working on the donkey machine when we noticed Dave, our faller, walking out of the bush. He had just bought a new chain saw and he had been pretty happy to be using it that day. As he walked towards us, I could see he was dangling something on a string. I yelled, "What on earth have you got dangling on that string?"

"It's a $300 yo-yo," he replied. The spring on the new machine's recoil broke the first day. It didn't matter how bad things got, Dave could always see the funny side!

We worked in the area above Ganges for a good year before we moved our machine to other places. For several years we logged quite a bit of timber off several hundred acres of our own property. I hauled the timber through Fulford to the end of Morningside Road where I dumped the logs into the water. When we were putting logs in the water, we got $50 per thousand board feet. Now they're worth a few hundred dollars per thousand, but we were making good money at the time.

Cooperation

In those days, most of the loggers helped each other, but there was one that was never ready to lend a hand. One newcomer found this out the hard way. He told me that he had forgotten his peavey on a morning when he was booming. He went out and asked the fella who was booming next to him if he could borrow one of his peavies for the day. The logger said, "No way! You can borrow my wife, but you can't borrow my peavey!"

Ken and I were always glad to help out. One chap who was logging behind us up on Regional Hill above Fulford had some trouble once. He came down to ask for some help because his haul back line had broken and wrapped around the block at the top of a one hundred foot spar tree. He needed someone to go up and unwind the haul back line and throw it down so it could be mended. None of his crew would go up to untangle it, so he was hoping that Ken could help.

Ken was in Victoria, so I thought I might give it a try. "Have you got a pass line?" I asked. The pass line is a cable that's about 3/8th of an inch thick and it runs through a block to pull someone up the spar tree. You sit in a loop of chain that's attached to the pass line and hang on while they take you up to the top of the tree by moving the pass line.

"Oh yeah, I've got a pass line," he said with confidence, so I offered to go up and see if I could fix his problem.

When we got up to his setting, I could see that there was a wrap around the block with about twenty feet of loose cable hanging down. Unfortunately, it was the same cable that pulled the pass line. No wonder his boys wouldn't go up there—each man had good reason to be afraid that when the wrap was taken off the block, the loose pass line cable would pull through the block—and take him with it!

I decided to give it a try anyways. They pulled me all the way up the spar tree in that darn thing and it was sure nerve-wracking! That pass line wasn't wound onto the drum very tight and every once in a while the cable dropped off the coil and I bounced around up there around the tree.

Eventually I got up to the top and looked down. Boy, it was a long ways down! There was nothing but rocks down there so I didn't look down anymore. I just kept looking straight ahead at what I was doing. After a while I got the haul back untied off the block and dropped it for them. That was an experience!

☙ Me, standing in front of one of the big, first growth trees that was logged on Salt Spring Island. This log was wider than I was tall. (circa 1960s)

Parties

Speaking of experiences, Dave, our faller, was a good one for parties. Once he put on a birthday party for his wife Dee Dee. He told Ken and me that he was going to put on something special for Dee Dee and he asked us if we would come over on Saturday night to help celebrate.

When Ken and I got there, things were already underway. Dave invited us into the living room where there was a bunch of men sitting around playing poker. The game had a 10 cent limit, so no one could lose much—the added benefit was that it cut down on the fighting. Ken and I sat down to play and enjoyed the big fire roaring in the fireplace.

The birthday girl was in the kitchen, while the boys were drinking beer around the card table. It was near the end of the night when Dave called out for her to bring the boys some coffee and sandwiches. "They will be getting hungry," he said with encouragement. Soon, Dee Dee came in with a plate full of sandwiches and a big jug of coffee for us all.

Not long after the sandwiches had disappeared, Dave hollered out again to tell Dee Dee that it was time to put another log on the fire, as it was starting to get cold in the room. That was enough for Dee Dee. "Get the wood yourself, you old so and so!" she shouted.

Dave was hurt and reminded her that she had no cause to be so upset. After all, hadn't he just bought her a new fur coat for her birthday?

There was silence for a minute before Dee Dee whooshed into the room with her new fur coat bundled up under her arms. She didn't even hesitate when she threw it into the fire. The coat made a swish sound when it hit the hot coals.

High Rigging with a Hangover

Dave's falling partner, Pete, was also a high rigger. He would go to the top of a sturdy tree and place the rigging needed to use it as a spar tree to haul in the logs.

One Friday afternoon before a long weekend, Pete promised to rig a spar tree for us on the following Tuesday. Both Pete and Dave wanted their paycheques early that Friday. They were planning to have a party for their friends. We gave them each a cheque and, as they left, Dave reassured us that he and Pete would be ready early Tuesday morning to rig the spar tree.

On their way home they stopped at the Fulford Inn, backed their truck up against the delivery door and told the manager that they wanted to buy all the beer in the inn's cooler. The manager had about one hundred cases, but since he needed half of them for the hotel, he could only spare fifty cases. Dave told him that that would make a good start, so they loaded the cases onto the truck. As can be expected from this beginning, the party lasted all weekend.

On Tuesday morning Ken and I went down to get Pete so that he could rig the tree. He wasn't in very good shape, but said he would do the job. On our way to the site, Pete realized that he had forgotten his cigarettes, so he asked us to stop at the hotel so he could buy some more. After quite a few minutes of waiting, Ken and I went into the hotel looking for Pete. He was standing at the bar with three empty glasses in front of him and a half-full glass of beer in his hand. "Now I won't have to take any time off for lunch," was all he said. He finished his drink in a gulp and walked back to the truck with us.

By the time we got to the site, Pete was getting very unsteady on his feet. Ken suggested that we do the job the next day, but Pete was a big man and stubborn too. He wanted to do it then. He got into the pass loop at the end of the pass line and said he wanted to go ahead. With Pete secured inside the pass chain, Ken put the machine in gear and pulled Pete one hundred and twenty feet up to the top of the spar tree.

Pete threw his climbing belt rope around the tree, tied it to the opposite side of his belt, dug his spurs into the tree and, still sitting in the short chain that was attached to the pass line, decided to have a sleep. Ken and I were very worried, but since Pete was all hooked in up there and we had no way to get to him, we couldn't do anything but wait. About an hour later, Pete shouted down to Ken that he was going to take his advice and rig the spar tree on Wednesday.

Day to Day Logging

Lots of years the winter months were so wet that we couldn't haul our timber out of the settings. If the roads in the mountains got to be so muddy that we couldn't get our truck up there, we would just fall more timber in preparation for the spring.

When the roads dried out, we brought in the donkey to yard the logs before bringing them down to the harbour. With our gas donkey in place and all the lines hooked up in the right places, Ken would build a truckload on the ground and then rig it so I could drive the trailer under it.

The load of logs, which were anywhere from thirty to forty feet long, was laid out with the back end on a brow log that was four or five feet high. The front end of the load rested on the ground with a couple straps underneath. We always had another strap about a hundred feet up in a spar tree.

Using a block and tackle and the gas donkey's mainline for power, Ken lifted the front end up in the air about six or seven feet while I backed the truck in underneath the load, right to the brow log. The box of my truck was a little higher than the brow log and when we let the load down, the front end would rise up off the brow log and I'd drive away.

Lots of times we just kept trucking through the spring. Ken built the load; I took it to Fulford and dumped it. By the time I got back from the harbour, Ken would have another load ready for me to load up and truck out again. I could take five or six loads to the harbour each day.

I was by myself on the truck and we had a small Fordson tractor that we called the 'dump machine' at the beach. I had to crank it to get it started. Boy, it was cold in the morning trying to get that thing going! I put straps under the load and released the stakes on the bunk and the logs fell down towards the water, onto the brow log. Then I went ahead with our little machine to pull the straps underneath the pile of logs. They rolled right over the brow log and down into the water.

ଓଃ My children, Morris, Cathy and Dan, helped me with my logging work occasionally. (circa 1954).

Floating the Jackpot

Sometimes, when the tide was out during the day, the logs piled up pretty near the brow log and at night when the tide came in, we had to float the jackpot into a pocket. We joined several big logs, called boom sticks, together into a long line and tied both ends to the beach so the boom sticks created a floating pocket in water that was about thirty feet deep. We got a tugboat to hook on to the jackpot's key log and to drag the whole thing into deep water. There might have been ten loads of logs in the jackpot by that time. It would have been piled up about forty feet high, just like a huge beaver's nest. Logs everywhere!

After the tugboat had pulled the jackpot into the pocket, we broke it up until it was flat on the water. Ken and I walked out on the boom sticks and used a peavey, a five foot long handle with a hook on the end, to roll the logs off the pile. Even though we wore boots with little nails on the bottom to grip the logs, it was dangerous work because the jackpot could break too fast and the logs would just go everywhere! If you fell into the water, you could end up trapped under the logs.

One morning when we had to break a jackpot in the booming grounds, we had a young fella just out of high school helping us. He was quite scared when the logs started to roll because he didn't know how to swim. He asked Ken what he should do if he fell into the water. Ken told him to hold on to his peavey: "It will take you to the bottom of the bay and then you can walk ashore." The bay was about thirty feet deep! The poor fella fell in a few times, but someone was always there to pull him out of the water.

Boats

I've loved water and boats ever since I was a young boy. Every once in a while, Grannie and I paddled over to visit Chief Charlie and his wife at the Indian reserve out of Fulford. Chief Charlie always took me to his long house where he kept his canoes. I admired his collection, but I had my eye on a short canoe that I suspected would go really fast. Chief Charlie always said he'd give me one of his canoes, but definitely not the one that I wanted. "I'll give you any of the other bigger safer canoes," he said, "but I won't give you that one. You'll drown yourself!"

He was saving those canoes and a lot of money and things for his last potlatch. He was planning to invite the chiefs from all the tribes around the area, but he never got the chance.

He and his wife were both murdered. They were ambushed on their way home from the store at Beaver Point. His canoe was found awash on Portland Island. Somebody knew he was saving money for the potlatch and, although they didn't take the canoes, many of his things were stolen.

Chief Charlie saved me from that fast canoe, but I managed to get myself into some boat trouble anyways. One morning, Ken and I were working out in Maxwell Bay when the battery on the boom winch went down. When we couldn't get it started, Ken asked me to go around in the boat to get the battery recharged.

I had a pretty fast speedboat. It was a very light narrow boat with a fifty horsepower Evinrude motor that went between twenty-five and thirty miles per hour. I could swing that thing and it'd turn right around on a dime!

It had rained the night before and water had collected under the boat's floorboards. I never noticed the water in the boat, so when I got it going full speed alongside the boom, I turned the boat sharply. All the water under the floorboards moved to one side and she just flew up in the air and flipped. I couldn't hold on and flew through the air too!

I had no idea what would happen to the boat. I came up for air, shook my head and looked around. The boat was upside down with the prop sticking up in the air. The motor must have stopped as soon as it hit the water. It wasn't a pretty sight, but I was glad to see it! I would have had some trouble if that boat had righted itself again. It would have gone around in circles and I would have been dodging it for half an hour!

As it was, I swam up to the boat, crawled up onto its bottom and waited. Ken had seen everything and ran to borrow a neighbour's boat. By the time he got to me, I had been in the cold water for half an hour.

Chief Charlie probably wouldn't have been surprised to hear that I had gotten into so much trouble with a fast boat!

16
Building Community

I'VE ALWAYS ENJOYED SALT SPRING ISLAND, and the Fulford community in particular. I've enjoyed many dances, ball tournaments and picnics, among other events that were organized by volunteers who put in many hours of hard work for the benefit of the entire community. It was only natural that I'd pitch in my services when I could to return the favour and to ensure that the island remains an exciting and enjoyable place for us all to live.

Through my volunteer work I met and worked alongside many smart, hard-working and generous people. I've had some wonderful experiences and I've seen some great opportunities. Some of them came to pass and some of them are notable only because they hint at what might have been. Regardless of how things turned out, I am always impressed by the generosity of people.

Lost Opportunity

Mr. John Maxwell went looking for gold in Barkerville around 1860 and made pretty good money—enough to buy about eleven hundred acres of the Burgoyne Bay area. He married a Cowichan girl, Mary, and they raised four boys and a girl: Sam, Dick, Dave, Jim and Mary.

When John Maxwell died, he left the East half the property to his son Dick and the other half, including the Burgoyne Bay area, to his youngest son, Jim. It was said that he left $9,000 to each of the other children.

When the First World War came, Jim left for England to fight the Germans. Before he left, he willed his land to his sister Mary. After the war, Jim travelled by boat to visit his relations in Ireland, but he went missing during the trip. Jim was always a flashy dresser and it was suspected that someone, thinking he had money to steal, tossed him overboard on route to Ireland.

Because Mary had moved to California by this time, she let Dick farm her part of the property along with his own until 1939 when she sold it to a wealthy miner.

The Larson Farm

Mr. Louie Larson, from Spokane, Washington, was the multimillionaire who bought the Maxwell farm. He had made a lot of money on copper mining and spent $15 thousand of it to buy the farm. That was quite a bit of money in those days! Even though he was a millionaire, he was just an ordinary fella at heart and he was much loved by the community.

He used to sail his big yacht up the coast and into Burgoyne Bay when he wanted to visit the farm. His wife didn't like him being away from Spokane so long, so she bought a yacht of her own so she could sail up too! When they were both here, they each had a yacht—with full crews—moored in Burgoyne Bay. Mrs. Larson usually stayed for about a week or so before she and her crew sailed back to Washington.

Mr. Larson loved farming; he did so for a good many years and did very well with it. And he should have, he spent thousands of dollars fixing up the place: new barns, machine sheds, new fences and more. He built three new houses, kept a crew of men year-round to work on the farm and raised a herd of about fifty purebred Poll Angus cattle. He bought nothing but the best—including Dick Maxwell's property next door and a large area east of Lee's Hill that belonged to the Furness brothers.

The Furness property was quite rough, so Mr. Larson hired Mr. Brooks to come in with his bulldozer to clear some land. After about a month's work, Mr. Brooks was concerned enough to advise Mr. Larson that his bill was getting quite high. Mr. Larson told him to keep going. "You can't break me!" he said.

Mr. Larson was very well respected in the community. He was always ready to help anyone in need. After he passed away in the early 1950s, his widow came back every once in a while to visit their daughter, who lived here permanently.

Salt Spring Island Marine Park

A few years after Mr. Larson died, our local Liberal representative, Earl Westwood, called a meeting in Mahon Hall in Ganges and explained that the Federal government wanted to buy a marine park for Salt Spring Island. Mr. Vic Jackson, Mr. Gigerich and myself were asked to look around the island for a piece of property suitable for a marine park.

The three of us had a short meeting and decided that Jackson and Gigerich would look over the Ganges area and I would look at the property at the South end of the island. My first thought was of the Larson estate.

The Larson Estate

I knew the area very well. It was the land my great grandfather's people lived on many years ago. And, only a year before, I had helped cruise the timber in the area for a log buyer. We cruised ten million feet of old growth timber, worth millions of dollars at that time.

I thought eleven hundred acres around Burgoyne Bay would make a good park. The other two chaps thought Burgoyne Bay was fine, so we went to the 'powers that be' and told them about the idea. They also approved, so I went to talk to Mrs. Larson. She agreed to get her daughter and son-in-law together so we could talk about it.

Her daughter lived in a house on the hill on the main road, before Burgoyne itself. One afternoon we had tea on her lawn. I told her about the government's plan to buy a marine park for Salt Spring Island and explained that we were hoping we might be able to buy the farm. I could see that Mrs. Larson and her daughter were quite excited about the idea and quite willing to sell the property.

Mrs. Larson offered to sell the property, including all the land, the cattle and the machinery for $90,000, with only one request. She wanted the park to be named in tribute to her husband: The Louie Larson Memorial Marine Park.

This was an excellent price—especially considering the machinery, the cattle, the value of the timber and the improvements that had been made to the property. I knew that this was a great opportunity for the island.

If this deal went through, Salt Spring would own eleven hundred acres of land and ten million feet of timber, much of it old growth. My goodness, there was so much timber on the land that if the government were to have sold just a little corner of timber off the property, it would have paid for the whole place! I was anxious to get the deal done.

Mr. Larson's executor, Mr. Jenson, lived in Spokane, Washington and I needed to negotiate through him. Within days Mrs. Larson had made arrangements for me to meet Mr. Jenson at the Georgia Hotel in Vancouver.

I told Mr. Jenson about the conversation I had had with Mrs. Larson and his only comment was, "If Mrs. Larson wishes that the property become the Louie Larson Memorial Marine Park, that's the way it will be." The executor told me to get it started on my end and that he would carry it through until the transfer was complete.

Portland Island

When I came back to Salt Spring to share the good news, I was surprised to learn that the government had already bought Portland Island for the Salt Spring marine park.

Mrs. Larson was very disappointed when she learned that the deal could not go through. She very much wanted to contribute towards the Louie Larson Memorial Marine Park for the community, but that's the way it went.

After buying Portland Island from some local people, the government turned it over to Princess Margaret as a gift. She then gave it back to the province as a park. It's not developed at all, but people can boat over to look around. The purchase was not as good for the Salt Spring people as it could have been.

When Mrs. Larson couldn't sell the farm to the government for a marine park, she sold it to Prince Johannes von Thurn und Taxis from Germany for considerably more money than the amount for which she had agreed to sell it to the Canadian government. The prince held the property until recently when his widow sold the land to Texada Land Corporation.

We have had all sorts of trouble with this land, but it could have been a beautiful park that would have benefited the entire province. This is particularly disappointing to me, knowing the importance of this land to my ancestors.

Drummond Park

Fortunately we had better luck establishing a playground for the Fulford Valley kids in the late 1960s. One day I got the idea of trying to get a piece of waterfront for the young people of Fulford. There wasn't much waterfront left and the best piece that I could find was the land that had always been known as Jackson's Beach, which belonged to Mr. Few—or so we all thought!

Jackson's Beach

Mr. Walter Few had bought a several hundred acre parcel of land that had belonged to Mr. Tom Jackson. One day I asked Mr. Few if he would consider selling a piece of the waterfront for a park, but he didn't want to divide his land.

When I noticed that some of the fences on the property crossed in a way that didn't make any sense, I remembered something Dad had mentioned. In the early days, two previous owners, Mr. Shepherd and Mr. Soule, had traded some property. That got me thinking.

A few days later I was in Victoria and called into the Legal Survey office to see a friend of mine, Mr. Salmond. After I explained the situation to Mr. Salmond, he offered to look into it for us. About a week later, he phoned to tell me that the piece of property I wanted for the park actually belonged to Captain Drummond, Mr. Few's neighbour!

To be absolutely sure, Mr. Salmond offered to survey the land free of charge through the Legal Survey branch. For about three days I worked with Mr. Salmond to survey the properties and to figure out why there was confusion over the property lines.

In the early days Mr. Soule owned all the waterfront in the area. Mr. Jackson bought some inland property from Mr. Soule's neighbour, Mr. Shepperd. Some time later, Mr. Jackson traded five acres at the back of his property for two hundred and forty feet of Mr. Soule's waterfront. Somewhere along the line there must have been a mistake in their measurements because Mr. Jackson ended up with a fence around more property than he owned.

Years later, when Mr. Few bought the Jackson property, the fence was still in the wrong place. Although no one knew it at the time, part of Mr. Few's land belonged to his neighbour. By this time his neighbour was Captain Drummond. Everybody thought Mr. Few owned all the land within the fence line, but he didn't. I guess he just owned the fence!

Captain Drummond also believed that the fence dividing his land from the Few property was the real property line. When I visited Captain Drummond, I explained that we wanted the land by the water, better known as Jackson's Beach, for a kids' park. He looked at me kind of funny and said, "Well, I can't give it to you. It belongs to Mr. Few."

"No, I don't think it does," I said. "I think you own that land."

"Well, if I do own it, I'll give you part of it for a playground," he said.

So I said, "OK, that would be fine."

Drummond Children's Playground

It took me about two years to get it all straightened out. And it was tricky work because, although Captain Drummond wanted to give his land for the Fulford children's playground, he didn't want anyone to know anything about his involvement. He was quite a private fella and he stressed that this arrangement was just between him and me.

In our negotiations, Captain Drummond stipulated that he was donating the land for a children's playground—not for a park. He wanted it to be called the Drummond Children's Playground and this condition was put in writing and, eventually, given to the Fulford Hall Committee.

At that time, I was working through the Fulford Hall Committee and I knew that the committee would take over control of the playground in the end, but I couldn't tell them about it. For years, they didn't even know we were working on a playground. Everything had to be cut and dried and signed and sealed before I could tell anyone. There was so much legal work—back and forth to Victoria—but when Captain Drummond got the letter from the survey, he kept his word and donated part of his field for a children's playground.

This photo of Captain Drummond, surrounded by some of the children that enjoyed playing in his playground, was taken at the party that was held to thank him for his generous gift to the community. Although I'm sure there are more, I recognize children from the following families: Akerman, Kitchen, Lee, Mollet, Moulton, O'Donnell, Patterson, Rees, Roland, Simard and Tara. (circa 1960s) Photo credit: *Gulf Islands Driftwood*

Lots of local people spent many hours working to create the playground for the children. Mrs. Loretta Roland helped a lot with the paperwork. Ray Simard spent many hours clearing and leveling the land with his equipment. I remember that the Lees, Moultons, Kitchens, O'Donnells, Taras, and Akermans helped out in some way or another. I know that many more people helped, but unfortunately I just don't remember their names anymore. I do know that the community really pulled together and did a lot of work to make this a special place for the children to play.

The playground was so popular that it became too small within a couple of years. I thought we might be able to buy some more land from the Drummond family, so I talked to

Mr. Black, the Minister of Parks, about that possibility. He had a look and agreed that it was a real good piece of property. When he asked me how much I thought the land might be worth, I suggested about $2,000.

Captain Drummond had passed away by this time, so I visited his wife, Betty. “We’re having quite a time with that little park down there,” I said. “It has become so popular that it isn’t big enough for everyone who wants to use it. I wonder if we could buy the other part of your land and join it on to the part Captain Drummond gave us?”

Mrs. Drummond said, “Oh yes, that can be arranged. I’ll donate the rest of the land to that park and you can have the whole thing.”

I tried to talk her into selling it, but she wanted to donate it for the community. I didn’t want to say “You can give the cheque back to us,” but I reminded her that she could do whatever she wanted with the government’s money. I think she might have caught on.

She agreed to take the money and, as soon as she got her cheque, she gave it to the Fulford Hall Committee and we put it in the bank. The interest on that $2,000 still goes towards keeping up the park.

Fulford Hall

Fulford Hall has been the centre of community life here in the valley for as long as I can remember.

First Hall

The Fulford Women’s Institute raised the money to build the first hall in the early 1920s. The money was raised through card parties, dances and other events. The local farmers also donated money and labour to build it. Once it was finished, they used the hall for dances, concerts, card parties and basketball. That hall burned down a few years after it was built, much to the disappointment of the community.

Second Hall

The second hall was built soon after, in 1926. It was much larger than the first hall and had a high ceiling that made it a lot better for basketball. This is where we brought a lot of teams from Victoria, Saanich and Duncan for basketball games and dances. When the second hall burned down, we didn't have another in Fulford for a few years. During that time we had to go to Ganges for our games and dances.

Third Hall

Jack Graham, a neighbour of ours, built the third hall in 1948 and it's still standing. Jack had a good lot of local help to put up the frame. He thought the hall was very important for the community and volunteered several hours each day after his own work was done. He was one of the best community men on the island in those days. I think he worked too hard and passed away too soon.

The third hall served the community well for a few years, but there were some problems.

In the 1940s my aunt, Mrs. Carry Gyves, approached me about joining the Hall Committee because there was tension between some of the committee and some of the young people. Things had gotten so bad that there was even talk about closing down the hall. I discussed it with my friend Jack Roland, who was a very community-minded fella, and we decided that something had to be done to fix the situation. I attended the next hall meeting and was made Chairman of the Building Committee.

Roller Skating

I had heard of a roller skating club in Salmon Arm that wanted to sell all of their skates and equipment. Jack and I thought roller skating would be good for the young people, so I phoned the people in Salmon Arm. When they offered us a good deal, I drove to the Interior and brought home more than one hundred pairs of skates and lots of equipment. In no time, the kids were skating and playing hockey. Molly started a skating club that was very popular with the adults too. Our only drawback was that there was no place to sit and watch the skating.

Renovations

Now that it was being enjoyed by the community, Jack and I spent the next eight years upgrading Fulford Hall, with the support of the Federal Government's Winter Works program.

If the Hall Committee supplied the materials, the Winter Works program would pay the wages of up to ten people to work on the project for six weeks each year. Fortunately we had lots of jobs that fit the government's criteria. Salt Spring Island benefited from eight years of Winter Works funding and Fulford Hall received a much needed renovation. Jack and I donated our Winter Works wages back to the Hall Committee to help pay for the materials we needed.

Our first project put seating in the hall so that people could watch the roller skating. A carpenter named Mike Sober estimated the material we needed for a forty by twenty-four foot stage to be built above some living quarters that we had intended to offer to the building's caretaker. I approached the mills and lumberyards in Victoria for supplies and got most of it donated. Dave Pallot and Don Reynolds did all the electrical wiring and plumbing for free. We finished the job in six weeks. It was a successful group effort by lots of involved and committed donors and volunteers.

And with that we began a long-term effort to upgrade the hall and provide many years of use to the community.

The second year of Winter Works funding supplied the labour to put down a new maple floor, which was donated by the Lions Club.

The third Winter Works project enlarged the kitchen in the basement. Several men with wheelbarrows and shovels took out the old floor and the dirt underneath it. We laid down six inches of rock screenings and poured four inches of cement for a nice floor.

The fourth Winter Works project finished off the basement kitchen with a new sideboard, sinks and cupboards. We also finished the walls with hardboard and built a lean-to kitchen on the upstairs main floor. This was handy when the hall committee put on our fundraising dinners for the public. The $1.50 per plate helped to pay for our renovations.

The fifth Winter Works project built the lean-to entrance on the west end of the hall, including a balcony where people could watch roller hockey games. Building the forty-five by twenty-five foot entrance wasn't as much work as moving the restrooms that had been in the main hall out to the north wall of the entrance and then putting down a maple floor where they were.

Our sixth Winter Works project finished all forty-two thousand board feet of walls and ceiling in the main hall and entrance.

We painted the ceiling and the walls the seventh year and painted the outside of the building our last year with the project. With all that work done, Fulford Hall is still in good shape and serves the community well.

It was very satisfying to work with so many people who had the good of the community in mind. I hope that Fulford Hall will continue to provide young people with the same sort of enjoyable memories that it gave me and my friends while we were growing up.

17

The Akerman Family Museum

I OFTEN THOUGHT I'D LIKE TO HAVE A MUSEUM. I wanted to do something to honour Grannie for all the good things she did for me when I was growing up and I thought that a museum would be a good way to share the many interesting things I had collected over the years.

Akerman Family Museum on Fulford-Ganges Road. (circa 2001)

Indian Artifacts

Dad had collected quite a lot of objects when he was road foreman. When he was clearing land, ploughing fields or building roads along the beaches where the Indians lived, he would pick up artifacts, bring them home and store them in stumping powder boxes that he kept in the barn. Eventually, he had a big pile of stones, Indian tools and memorabilia. He thought I might like to have them, so one day he told me to take them home. I held on to them for many years with the idea that I might be able to do something special with them one day.

Dolls

While I was collecting Indian artifacts, Molly had her own collection. She liked babies so much that after our eleven kids grew up she began collecting dolls.

Molly used to buy old dolls and give them to her sister Peggy, who was a collector. After a couple years of that, I suggested she should start a collection for herself. She used her old age pension to buy dolls. Over about eighteen years she collected more than one thousand of them.

Some of the dolls were made before the turn of the century. She fixed the broken ones, mended their dresses and combed their hair. They looked like new when she was finished with them!

Molly belonged to several doll clubs and attended their shows and sales. She went to Vancouver, Victoria...anywhere there was a doll sale, she would be there!

Building the Museum

I was eighty when I decided that the time had come to build the museum. Molly was getting too many dolls for the space we had in the house, so one day I said to her, "Maybe I'll build a museum and move my Indian artifacts from the gymnasium into the museum. That way, you can put all your dolls in the playroom."

Molly said, "I'll believe it when I see it!"

Crazy Horse Martin

I was very lucky to have a good friend by the name of Crazy Horse Martin volunteer to help me. His real name is Lorne Martin, but everyone calls him Crazy Horse. He's the best log builder in BC and a good man with the chain saw. He was very busy, but he offered to help me in his spare time.

Crazy Horse told me to get the logs out of the woods, peel off the bark and get them down to the spot where I wanted to build. The next day I sharpened my chain saw and put on my hard hat.

When Molly asked what I was doing, I explained that I was going to get some logs for the museum. She couldn't believe I was really going to go through with it and said she would come and take a picture of me falling the first tree.

I felled sixty trees in all. Val, a friend of ours who had played on Molly's ball team, helped me take the limbs and bark off the trees. Then I got a self-loading truck and hauled the trees to the building site.

A young carpenter who rented from me put the forms in for the cement foundation and my sons poured the cement. Then it was Crazy Horse's turn.

He had an A-frame—a machine that lifts logs—at his place in Duncan. It was made of an old car, but that A-frame worked just like a crane. Crazy Horse used it to pick up logs and place them anywhere he wanted. It was in pretty bad shape, though: the tires were no good and it had no brakes.

Of course, Crazy Horse couldn't get it licensed. He knew it wasn't legal, but since he wanted to get it over here to help with the museum, he left Duncan really early in the morning and took the back road to the Crofton ferry. He got half way when a young RCMP officer stopped him.

The cop got out of his car and looked suspiciously at the contraption. He couldn't figure out what it was. He tried to test the brakes and could tell that there were none. Then he noticed that the tires were all bald. He took his book out and started writing all these things down. I guess he was thinking he would write Crazy Horse a ticket. After a while, when he had pretty well a page worth of problems written down in his book, he asked, "Where are you taking this thing anyways?"

Crazy Horse said, "Well, I'm taking it to Salt Spring to help a friend of mine build a museum." The young cop scratched his head.

"Well," he said, "I haven't got enough pages in my book to charge you for everything, so you take it over to Salt Spring and you leave it there!"

So the cop let him go and Crazy Horse came over here with his contraption and helped me build the museum. It sure saved a lot of heavy lifting. It took us three months, off and on, to build the museum.

My daughter Roberta met Crazy Horse for the first time when he was building the museum. She introduced herself and told him that she was pleased to meet him because she had heard a lot about him. "I hope it was all good," Crazy Horse said.

Not being one to shy from the truth, Roberta admitted, "Some good. Some bad."

That Crazy Horse Martin was a colourful guy! He could sure swear—every other word out of his mouth was a swear word. And it was awfully hard to keep him working because his friends always came along and invited him to have a beer. He always went with them down to the pub and that was the last I'd see of him for the day! He got in only a couple hours of work each day, but he was a genius when it came to using a chain saw. I enjoyed having him around and I was glad to have his help, that's for sure.

Crazy Horse did most of the work on the museum and, when he was done, he took the A-frame back to Duncan. I didn't ask him how he got it back, but it's over there now.

Roofing

My brother Jim and I split the shakes for the roof and put them on. Not bad for eighty and eighty-four year old guys! People shouted as they passed along the road "Get down off there you crazy so and sos! You'll fall off and kill yourselves!" I think people were glad when we got finished.

After we got the museum built, I moved my artifacts to the museum and Molly put all her dolls in the gymnasium, just like I said would happen!

☙ Here is Molly with some of her dolls in the old gymnasium. (circa 1980s)

☙ Molly's dolls. (circa 1980s)

Visitors

I didn't put up any signs to tell people about the museum, but they started to come anyway. I get school kids by the busload and tourists drop by in all manner of transportation. Once a vintage car club visited and they parked fifty or so old cars in my driveway!

I've had more than a hundred people here at one time to see the Akerman Family Museum. Some people hear about it from the folks at the Salt Spring Information Bureau and others must hear about it through word of mouth.

People who want to come here just call me on the phone to let me know they're coming. I meet them at the door and show them around. It's that simple, but people are always asking about the museum's hours. I've been thinking of saying "It's open when it's open and it's closed when it's closed."

I don't ask anyone to pay admission, but a notice on the door says, "By Donation." Most people put money in the bucket. Very often, people with old beat-up cars put in more money than those with fancy cars.

Questions

The visitors always have questions to ask. Of all the people that come here, I find that the city people ask the craziest questions. Some of them don't know much about the country, that's for sure. Although they think the island is beautiful, they can't understand why my grandparents would have wanted to come here to live. They figure no one would want to leave the city to start a new life in the wilderness.

I always explain what you already know: my ancestors couldn't afford land in the old country and they heard they could get it here for a reasonable price. They came here to look for a way to make a living and they found a wonderful place to live.

I don't tell those city folk about the beautiful weather, or the strong sense of community or the fact that we could live off the land when people in other parts of the country were starving. I certainly don't bother to mention that the cities are way too crowded! I don't argue with them at all about the best place to live, but of course I prefer Salt Spring Island.

Those city folk are real good people and I wouldn't want to upset them, but when they can't understand why people would want to live on Salt Spring Island, I think they're just a little dumb in some ways.

The End

18

The Fulford Valley

I have never spent a day working for the man
I've lived my life on Salt Spring Island, Fulford Valley, south end
Carved out a home here with my family, got our needs met close at hand
All in all it's been a good life and I'm grateful to this land

And I will stay in the Fulford Valley
Like my father and his father before me
My roots go deep like the Cowichan in me
And I will stay in the Fulford Valley

Sometimes they ask me 'bout the old days and the old time pioneers
How they cleared and broke this land here with their blood, sweat and tears
Life was hard back then but simple though I've seen changes through the years
When my last sun sets on Mount Maxwell you can bury me right here

And I will stay in the Fulford Valley
Like my father and his father before me
My roots go deep like the Cowichan in me
And I will stay in the Fulford Valley

Words and Music by Alan Moberg
© 2001 Meadow Mountain Music

ɞ Me and Alan Moberg, who kindly wrote this song about me and my ancestors. (circa 2002)

19

A Different Perspective

IN THE PROCESS OF COLLECTING THE STORIES FOR THIS BOOK, I spent a lot of time reminiscing with my family. We've had some great times sharing stories and memories. We'll keep most of them to ourselves, but my children thought that some of them should be shared.

In the spirit of continuing the Akerman family history through to future generations, here are some of my children's memories. I hope that their children, grandchildren, and so on will read these and be inspired to add their own stories to the collection so that generations of our family will have a written connection to their past.

It Wasn't the Cat!

By Jim Akerman

One night, when I had stopped by Dad's for a visit, I was out in the back room getting The Driftwood *when I heard something crashing around and making a lot of noise in the basement. Assuming that it was Dad's cat down there, I joined Dad in the living room and started to read the paper.*

A story about some people seeing a bear on Salt Spring caught my eye. I asked Dad if he thought it was true and he said he didn't think so.

Not long after that, I noticed some cars stopping and looking in towards the front lawn. I mentioned it to Dad and we both got up to see what the excitement was about, but my truck was parked in the way, so we couldn't see what they were looking at. Dad jokingly said, "They're probably looking at the bear."

Dad followed me to the porch to see what was out there. I went to the driveway to have a closer look, but didn't see anything except a trail through the tall grass around the side of the garage. Dad went to the back porch, thinking that a deer had probably gone through to the back yard.

I was following the trail down by the garage, when Dad came back to the front porch and shouted down to me that he had seen a bear running around the back of the house. I must have been close to it when I was walking down by the shed. I went around the house and stood on an old barrel so that I could see down towards the creek. I didn't see anything, but I heard something splashing through the creek.

I wanted to see the bear for myself, so I ran over to the ball field where I knew the trail came up from the creek. The bear came straight up the trail. When he saw me, he shook his head, grunted and ran back up the creek. I knew then that the noise I heard in the basement wasn't the cat!

First Day of Hunting Season

By Ted Akerman

When I was about fourteen, Dad took us all up to Cape Kepple to drive sheep. While we were out on the range, we saw a big buck and decided we would bring it home.

We got up early on the first day of hunting season with our hearts set on getting that buck. On our way to a hilltop to look for it, we met a hunter who had come over from Sidney. Sure enough, he had already shot our deer. We were disappointed, but we kept going.

In no time, we saw a big two-point buck and a young spike. When we saw this big one, we were glad the hunter had grabbed the first deer and left this one for us!

We were up in the mountains, about a mile away from the truck, when Darlene got the spike and I shot the buck. That buck was huge—it weighed 156 pounds. It was big enough to win me the prize for heaviest buck at the Rod and Gun Club that year. Not bad for a fourteen year old. And I couldn't have done it without Dad's help.

Dad thought I was too young to carry a deer of that size, so he packed it all the way back to the truck for me while I carried Darlene's deer. Looking back on it now, I like to think I could have managed that big buck myself, but that I was just too smart to do it. It's the only story that makes sense—especially when I know that Dad was still packing deer out of the bush for me when I was thirty-five!

A Different Approach to Discipline

By Kerry Akerman

Dad had a different approach to discipline. One time, my brother Jim and I thought we would try smoking, so we took a couple of cigarettes from Mom's pack and snuck off down by the creek under the big cedar trees.

I don't know if Dad knew what we were up to or if he just heard all the choking and coughing, but he came down to investigate.

I noticed the look of fright on Jim's face even before he managed to blurt out "Look out! Here comes Dad!"

Jim tore off, jumped across the creek and hid up in the ball field. I was too slow. By the time I figured out what was going on, Dad was already there.

"What are you doing, Kerry?" he asked. I was still choking and coughing, so it was all I could do to look at him while he was talking.

"You're trying smoking, eh?" and he pulled a whole pack of cigarettes out of his pocket. With a funny smirk on his face, he offered the pack to me. "Here. You can have this whole pack of smokes."

I could barely get the words out, but I managed to say "No thanks. I don't think I'm going to try smoking again!" Jim got into more trouble for running away when he was told to stop than both of us did for smoking!

Where's My Smokestack?

By Patrick Akerman

One day when Danny and I were quite young, we found a couple of cigarettes and decided to try them out in the old barn. We each had one, but we were having trouble lighting them. Just as Dan got his going, we heard Dad coming into the barn. Dan threw his cigarette into the hay and disappeared. There I was, all by myself, with a cigarette in my mouth.

Dad walked right over. He was very serious when he said, "Let me feel your head." He felt around and ruffled my hair, as if he were looking for something. When he seemed convinced that everything was all right, he looked at me as if I was crazy and said, "Why are YOU smoking? You don't have a smokestack in the back of your head!" If God had meant for you to smoke, he would have put in a smokestack!"

I believed that for quite a while and never smoked again.

I Bless My Parents

By Cathy Cook (nee Akerman)

I remember Mom and Dad went away for a little trip and brought home gifts for us children. Each of the seven boys received rifle pop guns and the girls all got baby dolls. I was such a tomboy that I wanted a gun—not a doll. I was so disappointed that I cried until my brother Morry, who is two years older than me, gave me his gun. Mom gave my doll to some other little girl. I still remember the thrill having that gun and hunting with the boys. How hard it must have been for our parents to please each one of us!

Many times I have thanked God for our parents and for the love and care that they showed us children over the many years that they were raising us. What a job it must have been! With each passing year I appreciate them more and I am amazed at all that they did—and are still doing—for us. Having only four children of my own, it is hard to fathom raising eleven. I bless my parents.

The Best Fishing Pole

By Jim Akerman

When I was about four or five the land behind our house was cleared all the way down to the creek. One time I noticed some boys fishing down there.

I told Dad how I wished I had a fishing rod so that I could go down there and catch a fish for myself. Dad said, "If you want a fishing rod, I'll get you one like I used to use when I was a boy."

He cut a willow branch and tied a white string onto one end of it. On the end of the string, he fastened a safety pin. I remember that he had a difficult time finding a pin, so he borrowed one from Kerry's diaper!

Now that the pole was ready, he took me to the garden to dig up some worms. Down at the creek, he put one of the worms on the pin, threw the line into the water and gave the rod to me. No sooner had I took hold, than I got a strike. I pulled in what seemed like a big trout.

I noticed that the boys downstream were still fishing and hadn't caught anything with their fancy rods. I felt very proud to bring my fish home for Mom to cook for supper.

Memories of Special People in Our Lives

By Cathy Cook (nee Akerman)

Lance, the youngest of the Akerman children, was our most special gift from God. He taught us so much. Despite his mental challenges, which were probably caused by a lack of oxygen during birth, he was a beautiful happy child. Life was busy, but fun, when Lance was around. He now resides in a lovely home in Nanaimo, British Columbia.

Our house was always open to everyone from the local Catholic priest to sports teams. Our extended family included two foster brothers, Ronnie Pappenburger and John Barker, and of course our wonderful cousins: Daphne and Laurie Mouat; Ross and Sherrie Bryan; David, Clare, Pauline, and Peter Harris; Diane and Shelia Carlin; Marylou, Donnie, and Jane McTighe and Brenda and Roy Whitford; Terry and Wesley Akerman; Bruce and Carol Brenton; and many second cousins.

Mom and Dad's home could have been called The New Traveller's Rest!

Bush Duck

By Morris Akerman

When I was about ten years old, I had a pet duck with pink colouring on his face. We called him Bush Duck.

We used to take him way up the mountain behind the house to a place we called Grandview. After hiking thirty-five minutes to an hour on the mountain trails, we would toss Bush Duck off the cliff. He always flew right back to our house, where he waited for us to hike back down the mountain, pick him up and carry him back to the top of Grandview for another flight home. He seemed to enjoy it, so we would continue to travel back and forth between the house and the top of Grandview until we were too tired to walk up the hill again. I think he had the last laugh because he always seemed ready to go back again even though we were worn out.

One day, when Bush Duck was flying down to the house, an eagle decided that our duck would make a good duck dinner and tried to grab him. Bush Duck skillfully dodged the eagle and landed safely at the house. The eagle would not come near our house, so thankfully Bush Duck survived to fly another day.

Dad's 90th Birthday

By Darlene O'Donnell (nee Akerman)

On January 6, 2002 we had an open house to celebrate Dad's 90th birthday, which was the next day.

We had placed an announcement in the local paper, the Driftwood, *the previous Thursday, inviting family and friends to the open house at our family home. We did not tell Dad about it ahead of time because we knew that he would think it was a bad idea. When he saw the announcement in the* Driftwood, *he cried "No! No! No!"*

We had the party anyways. Two hundred people came through the house to wish Dad well. Everyone, including Dad, had a wonderful time. Dad was especially pleased to see some of the old-timers, including Mrs. Hepburn, Mrs. Twa, Mrs. Ruckle, Mrs. Mouat and more. Our relatives from the Cowichan First Nation gave Dad a beautiful carved mask and honoured him with an authentic Indian song and dance.

I made a display of Dad's life using little figurines to represent some significant times and people in his life. One small vignette showed Burgoyne Bay in the 1800s, with a teepee and a tiny baby that represented Dad's Grannie. There was also a little house that represented Traveller's Rest and a little figurine that represented Dad's Grandmother Akerman chasing a cougar away from baby Fanny, who was sleeping peacefully in a tiny apple box. One scene showed Dad meeting Mom and then another showed them getting married. Mom was shown taking care of her eleven children while surrounded by her ever-present pots, pans and canning supplies, while Dad was hard at work.

The display concluded with scenes of Dad's many community activities and his museum. It was fun to put together the display and to remember all of the interesting times in Dad's life.

ℭ Me at my 90th birthday party. (January 2002)

ଓ My second cousin, Ben George and his sons Robert and Larry at my 90th birthday party. (January 2002)

"I Guess I Loaded it a Little Heavy"

By Dan Akerman

The funniest story I remember about my dad happened about a quarter mile up hill from the stone church at Fulford, where I was using my bulldozer to clear some land for him.

Dad always liked to watch land being cleared and he came up to see how things were going. When he saw that I was having a little trouble pushing out a stump that was about six feet across, he started waving his arms for me to stop. He came up alongside the bulldozer and told me to clear the land further along. He would take care of the stump.

As he drove off in his jeep, I wondered what he was talking about, but I didn't ask any questions.

About a half an hour later I saw him backing his jeep up to the huge stump. He started unloading boxes and boxes of dynamite and fertilizer. I hoped he knew what he was doing. There were a lot of boxes.

After spending about an hour digging under the stump, he put all the dynamite in the hole. Except for a fuse that he left sticking out of the ground, he covered everything with dirt. Then he moved the jeep about 200 yards down the road and around the corner.

The next thing I saw was him lighting the fuse and casually walking up the hill to where I was working with the bulldozer. As he got up to me, he told me that I had better get off and get behind the dozer with him.

No sooner did we get behind the dozer than there was a huge explosion. The ground shook and when I peeked around the dozer, there was nothing but rocks and chunks of stump flying everywhere.

When the dust cleared, Dad and I walked down to where the stump used to be—and I mean USED to be! There was nothing there but a thirty foot wide and seven foot deep crater. Dad just looked at me, shook his head and said, "I guess I loaded it a bit heavy."

I walked Dad back to his jeep. When we came around the corner, we saw that its driver-side door was caved in right to the steering wheel. The culprit was the 50 pound chunk of stump laying beside it. Again, Dad shook his head and said, "I guess I loaded it a bit heavy."

This is not over yet.

When I got into my truck and drove home, past the stone church, there where chunks of stump and rocks all over the main road.

Of course, days later, when people asked Dad and me about the stuff on the road, we did not know anything about it.

Too Much of a Good Thing Can Kill You!

By Darlene O'Donnell (nee Akerman)

When I told Dad that I had Hereditary Hemochromatosis, he said " HemochromoWhat? Never heard of it!" Most people haven't heard of it. One in three hundred people are affected and one in seven are carriers. Mom and Dad had no symptoms, but were carriers. Many people in our family have been affected by this disease and I want them to know that help is available.

People with Hemochromatosis have toxic levels of iron, which damages the body's organs—especially the liver and heart.

Effective treatment, called phlebotomy, is available. Phlebotomy, which is much like giving blood to the Red Cross, reduces the strain on the body by removing excess iron from the bloodstream.

If diagnosis is made before organ damage sets in, hemochromatosis patients can live relatively normal lives.

Information is available from the Canadian Hemochromatosis Society at 1-877-BADIRON and www.cdnhemochromatosis.ca. Or just ask me—I'll be happy to tell you all about it!

A Good Shot

By Ted Akerman

Dad knew his way around the bush—and he was a good shot too. Once, I saw him aim at a pheasant on the fly and hit it in the head with a twenty-two. He remarked that they were easier to clean that way.

Another time, a bunch of us kids were walking up Musgrave Road to go drive sheep. Up a ways, we could see a grouse sitting on a rock. Dad threw a stone at the bird: it knocked him out and he fell off the rock. I ran up ahead of everyone else to pick up the bird and I pulled the head off before they got close enough to see. Then I ran up to them with the grouse in my hand and said, "Hey, look at this! Dad knocked the head right off it!" The kids were sure impressed that day.

Saved from the Bees

By Patrick Akerman

When we were driving sheep at Isabella Point, one of my jobs was to stand in the middle of a certain trail to stop the sheep from taking it.

I was the youngest out on the range and sometimes I got a little distracted. Once, while I was waiting for the sheep to come down the trail, I decided to sit down on a stump. Out of boredom, I guess, I started banging a rock on the stump, trying to break it apart.

I was just starting to make some progress when along came the sheep. Sure enough, with me sitting out of the way on the stump, they trotted right down the trail I was supposed to keep them from. Darlene was right behind them and I probably would have gotten into trouble, except that, at that moment, yellow jackets started swarming all around me.

Darlene started yelling, "Get out of there! It's a bee's nest!" I was so scared that I froze and refused to move. Darlene ran into the middle of the swarm, picked me up off the stump and carried me to safety.

I didn't even get one sting, but Darlene got quite a few. When she was swollen and sick for a few days afterwards, I felt bad knowing that she was hurt because of me.

Boogie Eyes!

By Kerry Akerman

Whenever Dad came back from a trip off the island, we would run to see what he had brought back. Usually, he would have a stick of Wrigley's spearmint gum for each of us.

Dad came home one day with a big farm truck. I ran out to the front porch to see him. He gave me a stick of gum and picked me up to show me what he had in the back of the truck. I was about two or three and had no idea what might be in there. I squinted my eyes and looked between the boards. I was sure surprised to see a pair of big scary eyes staring at me. "Ahh!" I screamed "Boogie Eyes!" If I had a diaper on, I'm sure I needed a change!

I don't think we had it for very long, but from that day on, the name stuck with the horse. He was pretty calm when Dad bought him, but Dad figured he had probably been drugged to keep quiet. After Dad got him home, he was a stick of dynamite!

Jingle Bell

By Roberta Allard (nee Akerman)

When we were young, Darlene, being the eldest, was given the responsibility to raise an orphaned lamb, whom she named Bambi. I thought Darlene was very lucky.

When a second orphaned lamb arrived, my older brother Ted was given the responsibility of raising her. I was extremely upset and cried about the unfairness of it all. Eventually, Ted felt sorry for me and gave the little lamb to me. I called her Jingle Bell; she was my pride and joy.

A year or so later Jingle Bell was put out to range with the other sheep. When we camped and drove our sheep into corrals at Cape Kepple, I would often see Jingle Bell there. She had a lamb each year for many years. And every year I saw that each of her lambs had lambs of their own.

Now, when I visit my brothers I remind them that I'll be coming back to claim Jingle Bell's offspring one day. It's been more than forty years now, so I expect to have a sizeable flock!

"That's fine with me," Ted always says, "but you can also expect to receive a sizeable bill for feed and care!"

Cougar in the Basement

By Kerry Akerman

As a small child, I was not allowed in the basement. I figured out later that it was because there were so many dangerous things, like tools and hunting equipment, down there and Dad didn't want us to get hurt. Rather than tell us the obvious, Dad told us that there was a cougar down there.

To prove the point one day, one of the older boys wrapped a cougar skin rug around himself and hid at the bottom of the stairs. Another brother told me to look in the basement, which I knew I wasn't supposed to do. I got about halfway down the stairs when I saw the cougar that Dad warned me about, lurking in the dark. I came tearing up those stairs really fast. That kept me out of the basement for a long time!

20

Akerman Family Genealogy

1.

Johnathon Akerman Married Anne Pearce.

Ann Pearce Chirton, England. Daughter of George Pearce. Married Johnathon Akerman.

- **i.** **Joseph Akerman** Born March 25, 1834 at village of Tamy, England. Married Martha Clay.
- **ii.** **Sister**
- **iii.** **Sister**

2.

Joseph Akerman Born March 25, 1834 at village of Tamy, England. Married Martha Clay on May 14, 1863 at Victoria, BC.

Martha Clay Born September 26, 1839 at Hinkley, Leicestershire, England. Sisters: Fanny and Emma Clay. Married Joseph Akerman on May 14, 1863 at Victoria, BC.

- **i.** **Fanny Akerman** Born November 22, 1865 at Victoria, BC.

ii. **Joseph Johnathon (Joe) Akerman** Born April 2, 1868 at Salt Spring Island, BC.

iii. **Mathilda (Tilly) Akerman** Born February 23, 1870 at Salt Spring Island, BC.

iv. **Martha Ann Akerman** Born December 15, 1871 at Salt Spring Island, BC.

v. **George Edward (Ted) Akerman** Born November 28, 1873 at Salt Spring Island, BC.

vi. **James (Jim) Akerman** Born September 1, 1875 at Salt Spring Island, BC.

vii. **Thomas (Tom) Akerman** Born July 16, 1877 at Salt Spring Island, BC.

viii. **William Francis (Bill) Akerman** Born June 21, 1879 at Salt Spring Island, BC.

3.

George Edward (Ted) Akerman Born November 28, 1873 at Salt Spring Island, BC. Married Ellen Gyves in 1898.

Ellen Gyves Born to Michael and Mary Ann Gyves (T̲uwahwiye') (date and location unknown). Married George Edward (Ted) Akerman in 1898.

i. **Melissa Francis (Molly) Akerman** Born November 5, 1901. Married Howard Carlin.

ii. **Dorothy Rita Martha Akerman** Born November 29, 1903. Married Bill Harris January 13, 1939.

iii. **Mary Margaret (Tilly) Akerman** Born October 31, 1906. Married Maurice McTighe.

iv. **James Edward (Jim) Akerman** Born August 20, 1908. Married Alice Whittaker.

v. **Robert Michael (Bob) Akerman**. Born January 7, 1912. Married Mary (Molly) Reed Morrison July 7, 1939.

Children: Darlene Akerman (married name: O'Donnell), Robert Edward (Ted) Akerman, Roberta Akerman (married name: Allard), Merilyn (Lyn) Akerman (married name: Andrews), Morris (Morry) Akerman, Catherine (Cathy) Akerman (married name: Cook), Daniel (Dan) Akerman, Patrick (Pat) Akerman, James (Jim) Akerman, Kerry Akerman and Lance Akerman.

4.

Robert Michael (Bob) Akerman Born January 7, 1912 Married Mary (Molly) Reed Morrison on July 7, 1939.

Mary (Molly) Reed Morrison Born October 27, 1919 at North Vancouver, BC to Frank Morrison and Beula Morrison (nee Reed). Sisters: Betty and Peggy. Married Robert Michael (Bob) Akerman on July 7, 1939.

i. **Darlene Akerman** Born April 30, 1940. Married Tim O'Donnell.)

Children: Patricia O'Donnell (married name: Byron), Daniel O'Donnell, Mark O'Donnell, Shane O'Donnell, and Keith O'Donnell.

Grandchildren: Amanda, Matthew and Tim Byron; Ryan, Brittanie, Abigail, Molly, Clare and Josephine O'Donnell; Sarah and Bridget O'Donnell; Brandon and Rory O'Donnell; and Trent and Carmen O'Donnell.

ii. **Robert Edward (Ted) Akerman** Born December 2, 1941. Married Donna Underwood.

Children: George Akerman, Kenny Akerman, and Dawn Akerman (married name: Sawchuck).

Grandchildren: Molly Akerman; Max Akerman; and Cheyenne, Wyatt, Colby and Zack Sawchuck.

iii. **Roberta Akerman** Born January 6, 1943. Married Max Allard.)

Children: Michael Allard and Lynda Allard (married name: Psaila).

Grandchildren: Jared and Kurtis Allard; Olivia and Rebecca Psaila.

iv. **Merilyn (Lyn) Akerman** Born July 22, 1944. Married Dennis Andrews.

Children: Rick Andrews, Jack Andrews, and Michelle Andrews (married name: MacConnachie).

Grandchildren: Larissa Andrews; Mariah and Brock MacConnachie.

v. **Morris (Morry) Akerman** Born May 31, 1947. Married Janice Girard.

Children: Rachelle Akerman, Jacqueline Akerman, Janine Akerman, and Joe Akerman.

vi. **Catherine (Cathy) Akerman** Born April 21, 1949. Married Dale Cook.

Children: Dean Cook, Lance Cook, Tamera Cook (married name: Shearon) and Tatum Cook (married name: Taker).

Grandchildren: Jacob and Hunter Cook; Brandon, Bailey, Mikayla and Morgan Cook; Lleyton Shearon; and Gabriella and Mary Taker.

vii. **Daniel (Dan) Akerman** Born March 28, 1951. Married Barbara Byron.

Children: Charlotte Akerman, Mike Akerman and Willy Akerman.

Grandchildren; Julianna and Daniel Akerman.

viii. **Patrick (Pat) Akerman** Born April 15, 1954. Married Brenda Underwood.

Children: Robert (Bobby) Akerman, Catherine (Cathy) Akerman (married name: George), Gordon (Gordie) Akerman, and Jennifer (Jenny) Akerman.

Grandchildren: Christopher and Taylor Akerman; Billy and Monica George.

ix. **James (Jim) Akerman** Born June 9, 1955.

x. **Kerry Akerman** Born July 16, 1957. Married Leah Pallot.

Children: Clayton Akerman and Cara Akerman.

xi. **Lance Akerman** Born November 9, 1958.

21

Gyves Family Genealogy

1.

___ Gyves

Wife

- **i.** **Michael Gyves** Born in Ireland. Married Tuwahwiye', christened Mary Ann Gyves before wedding ceremony.
- **ii.** **Jim Gyves**.
- **iii.** **John Gyves**

2.

Michael Gyves Born in Ireland, date unknown. Married Ellen Gyves.

Tuwahwiye' Birth date unknown. Born at Burgoyne Bay, Salt Spring Island, BC. Born to a hereditary chief of the Clem-Clemelutz clan of the Cowichan First Nation, Chief Tusilm. Christened Mary Ann Gyves. Married Michael Gyves.

- **i.** **Ellen Gyves** Married George Edward (Ted) Akerman July 7, 1898.

  Children: Melissa Francis (Molly) Akerman, Dorothy Rita Martha Akerman, Mary Margaret

(Tilly) Akerman, James Edward (Jim) Akerman, Robert Michael (Bob) Akerman.

ii. **Michael Gyves**

iii. **Mary Katherine Gyves**

22

My Native Ancestry

1.

Chief Tusilum Birth date and location unknown. Married T̲altunaat.

T̲altunaat Birth date and location unknown. Married Chief Tusilum.

- **i.** **T̲uwahwiye'** (Mary Anne Gyves) Birth date unknown. Born at Burgoyne Bay, Salt Spring Island, BC. Married Michael Gyves.

  Children: Ellen Gyves, Michael Gyves and Mary Katherine Gyves.

- **ii.** **Qwiyahwul't'hw** (son) Birth date unknown. Born at Burgoyne Bay, Salt Spring Island, BC. Married T̲litsiye'.

  Children: S'hwthilum (Alec George) and Slyelumul't'hw (Walter George).

- **iii.** **Kwulihwulwut** (daughter) Birth date unknown. Born at Burgoyne Bay, Salt Spring Island, BC.

Index

Page number references in bold include pictures.